'ic Quarte '.ib

Black Journalists, White Media

Black Journalists, White Media

Beulah Ainley

Trentham Books

First published in 1998 by Trentham Books Limited

Trentham Books Limited
Westview House
734 London Road
Oakhill
Stoke on Trent
Staffordshire
England ST4 5NP

British Cataloguing in Publication Data
A catalogue record for this book is available from the British Library
ISBN 1 85856 058 6
(HBK ISBN 1 85856 115 9)

Designed and typeset by Trentham Print Design Ltd., Chester and printed
in Great Britain by The Cromwell Press Ltd., Wiltshire

CONTENTS

FOREWORD

This book is the first of its kind in Britain dealing with black journalists as a group and their experiences of colour discrimination in the media. It is based on my Ph.D. study of 100 black journalists working in national and provincial newspapers, magazines, public relations, radio and television. My research was an attempt to look systematically at black journalists as a group, their backgrounds and experiences in education, the media and media unions and how they managed to get into a profession which in the main is closed to black people. It is also important to state that of those I interviewed, only 90 per cent agreed provided they were not identified for fear of losing their jobs. Some refused to be interviewed because the permission of their employers was withheld.

The term 'black' is used to cover people from the following ethnic groups: African, Caribbean, Asian and, because it is a political term, Chinese. While I recognise that there are cultural differences between these groups, all experience discrimination on the grounds that they are not white. Where the cultural differences are important I have discussed the groups separately.

Since the 1950s, the relationship between Britain's black population and the media, especially tabloid newspapers, has been hostile. The media have constantly portrayed black immigrants and their children in negative, stereotypical ways and as threats to white society: 'first through immigration and when settled here, posing a law and order problem' (Gordon and Rosenberg, 1989). Media racism has also found expression in the gross under-employment of black journalists in the white media. Yet the media have generally failed to put forward stories of prejudice, discrimination and deprivation experienced by black people. This is particularly evident in the reporting of what have been described as 'race riots'.

The controversy concerning race and the media led to a small number of academic researches including Hartman and Husband's *Racism and the Media* (1974), C. Critcher's *Race in the Provincial Press* (1975), Barry Troyna's *Public Awareness And The Media* (1981) and Teun A. van Dijk's *Racism and the Press* (1991). These studies found the media guilty of biased reporting on race. However, these researches concentrated on race reporting rather than the under-employment of black people in the media. Only Troyna (1981) mentioned black employment in the white media, when recommending that:

> Editors and the National Council for the Training of Journalists should actively encourage ethnic minority school leavers and graduates to enter journalism. This will not only help to provide equality of opportunity but will also contribute to the more informed and sensitive reporting of race issues (Troyna, 1981, 86).

There were some researches into journalists as a group, such as Jeremy Tunstall's *Journalists at Work* (1970) and Oliver Boyd-Barrett's *Journalist's Recruitment and Training* (1970), also Anthony Delano's *News Breed* (1994), but all dealt exclusively with white journalists .

In 1988 the National Union of Journalists (NUJ) estimated that 250 of its 28,000 members were black, less than one per cent. By 1997 it was 1.6 per cent but, although the numbers are rising, most black people who want to get into journalism are impeded because of discrimination. The nearest I found to a study of black journalists was a 1983 report by the Black Media Workers' Association. There have also been two books, *Black People and The Media* (1988) and Ionie Benjamin's *The Black Press in Britain (*1995), which looked at black people in the media, but they did not examine the situation of black journalists and the white media in depth.

ACKNOWLEDGEMENTS

I must first thank my Higher Power for the direction and strength given to me in order to complete this thesis. It was against all the odds that I did it. As a working-class, black woman I am rendered invisible by society's racism, sexism and class hierarchy.

Secondly, my thanks to the National Union of Journalists' Race Relations Working Party of the late-1980s, whose work inspired me to take on this project, and to those individuals in the Union, particularly Andrew Dixon and Sally Gilbert, who gave their time and effort in providing me with information. To the late Professor Alan Little, who not only encouraged my idea for this research but started me off. To Professor John Stone for his help and support throughout. I am also indebted to Professor Martin Bulmer of the London School of Economics and Political Science who provided help, guidance and constructive criticism. Special thanks to those journalists who willingly shared their experiences, giving me their valuable time.

Finally, to my husband Patrick, for his technical assistance and in particular my son Adam, hoping that this book will be another step in the struggle for equality and that he will grow up in a society where he will be judged by his skills and not the colour of his skin.

CHAPTER 1

RACE AND THE MEDIA

Introduction
The notion that the numbers of black journalists employed by national newspapers can fit into a telephone booth is not far from the truth. There are between 12 and 20 black journalists employed at any time by national papers, out of a total workforce of 3,000. The problem is even greater in provincial papers, a bastion of English racism. There are only 15 black journalists out of 8,000. This is less than one per cent – and Britain's black population makes up six per cent of the total population and, in inner-city areas such as London 15 per cent. This gross under-representation of black people in journalism makes a mockery of Britain as a multi-racial, multicultural society. However, this blatant discrimination by the British media is only a reflection of the structural racism which black people have experienced first in the colonies and later in the 'motherland'.

The relationship between Britain and black people began in the sixteenth century and was then and still is, based on the notion of white superiority. This belief was perpetuated by the media of the day in books and pamphlets used to justify slavery and colonisation.

But racism did not end after slavery or Britain's loss of empire. It was preserved in Britain's cultural heritage, with the zestful help of the media.

Immigration
When Black people were invited to Britain they were given what Ken Pryce described as 'shit work', low-paid, low status, the backbreaking jobs in the National Health Service, public transport and older

industries. These were jobs working-class whites did not want but they were deemed suitable for blacks who have historically been seen as fit only for menial tasks. The British government had no trouble filling its low-paid job vacancies. It had a 'reserve army' of labour in Africa, Asia and the Caribbean. The 'motherland' was well aware of the unemployment situation in these countries and knew that most black immigrants would be happy just to get a job rather than endure unemployment in their native country, and hope that things would change for them and their children in the future.

The newcomers experienced rejection and racial prejudice and were socially outcast from white society. It did not matter what skills they had, few were employed in white-collar occupations. There were, however, some journalists amongst the immigrants of the 1960s who had been trained in their own country but they too were expected to take unskilled jobs. White editors did not believe that black people had the ability to become journalists; some still do not believe it. Structural racism had educated editors and managers of the media to see black people as uneducated and unskilled, doing and deserving only labouring jobs. An African journalist told me of his experience seeking employment in the white media during the 1960s:

> I applied for over ninety jobs. I tried all the national papers except four. I informed all but ten that I was black. I received replies from these ten. Three offered me jobs in the provinces but because of the low salary I could not take them. The other seven had no vacancies. Of the 80 whom I informed I was black only 45 had the courtesy to reply. Some of those who did not reply went on advertising their vacancies for weeks afterwards. The standard reply from the 45 who did reply was that the post was already filled and that they would retain my application in their files should another vacancy arise in the future. Others said that they were seeking professionals from UK papers only. However, five replied saying that they did not have any vacancies at present but would like to meet me for future vacancies. I went but they were not serious about considering me for future employment. They just wanted to see what a black journalist looked like. I never did get a staff job on any of the papers. I had to settle for freelance work in order to live.

For most black immigrants in the 1950s and '60s journalism was not an option. They had to concentrate on survival, taking what jobs and housing they could get. Peter Fryer summed up the situation:

> prejudice against black people was widespread. More than two thirds of Britain's population held a low opinion of black people or disapproved of them. They saw them as heathens who practised head-hunting, cannibalism, infanticide, polygamy and black magic. They saw them as uncivilised, backward people, inherently inferior to Europeans, living in primitive mud huts in the bush. They believed that black men had stronger sexual urges than white men.

It was against this background of prejudice that black immigrants had to live. I remember the housing conditions I experienced when I came to Britain as a young girl in the 1960s. I had to share one room with three other relatives because no one would rent us a flat or house. The first house we lived in was cold and damp even in summer. It had seven rooms with at least three people living in each room. We shared one toilet, one bath and a three-burner gas stove. Cooking for all those people was particularly difficult, especially for families with small children. There were often disputes over the use of the stove and in the end most people lived on sandwiches and fish and chips.

I will never forget the day I saw a sign on a factory gate which read 'No blacks, no Irish wanted'. I asked my aunt what the sign meant and she explained as best she could but I was still puzzled as to why the factory did not employ Irish people – who are white. This my aunt could not explain; she was as puzzled as I was. It took several years before I was able to understand the full extent of racism.

Black people and the media

Although the relationship between Britain's black population and the media has been one of conflict, relations began on friendlier terms. In 1948, when the Empire Windrush landed at Southampton with 500 Jamaicans on board, the media welcomed them. It is difficult to imagine this happening in the 1990s. *The Daily Worker* headline read 'Five Hundred Pairs of Willing Hands' (June 23, 1948). This was followed up three weeks later by an article reporting that the Jamaicans had found homes and jobs and were settling down (July, 1948).

The London Evening Standard reminded its readers that many of those on the Empire Windrush had served King and country during the Second World War and that they were making a return to the 'Motherland', a fact which has since been conveniently forgotten. The media's welcome of black immigrants was maintained for ten years. So too was a self-imposed censorship regarding race-related stories. The media, especially the press, went out of its way not to report any aspect of race relations it saw as dangerous to racial harmony. This censorship was applied when, according to E.J.B. Rose, nearly 60 per cent of the white population saw immigrants as a 'threat' (Rose et al, 1969)

The media's self-imposed censorship also concealed the racism black people were experiencing, in the hope that it would go away. The idea was that focusing on racial problems would only make matters worse. However, the main reason for the media's silence about racism was that Britain needed cheap labour from its former colonies and did not want to create 'tension and adverse publicity' (Cashmore and Troyna, 1983).

The 1958 disturbances

In 1958 when white gangs attacked black people in Nottingham and Notting Hill, the media, especially the newspapers, dropped the pretence that black immigrants were 'welcome'. This uprising was to change how the media reported race-related stories. There were virtually no black journalists employed in the national press at the time, so the reporting was mainly from a white, racist perspective. The disturbances were the result of structural racism, media censorship on racism and the govern-ment's lack of financial support to local authorities with high concentra-tions of immigrants. Paul Foot noted that central government did nothing to help or to give any guidance from health or education ministries on the possibilities of different health and sanitation standards or on the difficulties of teaching children who could not speak English.

The Press reporting of the disturbances was sensational, insensitive and biased. It was easy to get the impression that it was black people who were rioting whereas it was whites (Hall, 1989). No in-depth analysis was offered to show the difficulties black immigrants faced in housing, employment and education, nor how they were invited here to help rebuild post-war Britain. Such hostile reporting sent a clear message to the black population that they were no longer wanted here and for those black people who had ambitions to become journalists, that they need not apply.

One newspaper which stood far above the rest was *The Manchester Guardian*. It not only reported the riots but gave space to black immigrants to articulate their views of life in Britain. In so doing, the paper presented both sides of the conflict so readers could make a more informed judgement of the situation. The paper rightly led some readers to question Britain being a just society. The 1958 riots exposed the 'government's lack of policy and its complacency on the subject of race relations' (Rose, 1969). However, the government's response was not to alleviate the social problems faced by immigrants in the decaying inner cities and thereby reduce racial tension, but instead, to bring in the 1962 racist immigration bill. There was no need for this Bill for, as Cheri Peach observed, 'migration was self-regulating; it rose and fell according to the demand for labour from year to year' (1963, 93).

Race reporting since 1958
Biased media reports about black immigrants and their children during and after the 1958 riots was to set the agenda for the next three decades. Gordon and Rosenberg (1989) observed that 'of all the domestic issues covered by the British press few have been so influenced and shaped by the press as the question of race'. The media did not use its influence and power to help create better race relations. Instead, its reporting on race issues perpetuated the notion of white superiority and the media in general, and tabloid newspapers in particular, show no inclination to do differently now. Though most newspaper editors will swear that their reporting is objective (one editor told me, 'We report the news as it is whether the subject is black or white'), this is far from the truth, as studies since the 1970s have shown. Media researchers Hartman and Husband (1974), Critcher, Parker and Sondhi (1977), Hall et al (1978), and van Dijk (1991) have found that the media, and especially national tabloids, continued to associate black people with problems or conflict, yet failed to pay attention to racism and violence against black people.

One example of the media's anti-black stance was shown in its support for the 1962 anti-immigration Bill and every anti-immigration Bill since. This Bill blamed black people – the victims of white racist attacks in 1958 – for Britain's 'race problem'. It was easy for the British public to support this view, as the media, especially national tabloids, made sure readers were given a distorted view of immigrants and immigration, portraying black people not as an integral part of British society but as 'some kind of aberration' (Hartman and Husband, 1974, 145).

The media's coverage of Enoch Powell's speech in 1968 was another illustration of the media stand on race. Powell's speech did nothing to benefit race relations but the press's saturation coverage of the speech was surely not only for its news value. Most national papers carried the story of Powell's racist sentiments for nearly two weeks. Yet they never did give such attention to incidents where black people were subjected to racist attacks or other forms of discrimination. Some papers criticised the speech, others did not. Their handling of the story was insensitive and their headlines emotive. *The Sunday Express* saw the speech as a 'Race Block Buster' (21/4/68) and *The Sunday Times* as 'Explosive Race Speech' (21/4/68). Although Powell was dismissed by the government, he received a great deal of public support. It is not that the people who supported him were born racists; their views are the product of structural racism and encouraged by the media.

Sensationalist racist reporting did not end with Powell's speech but intensified during the next two decades. By the 1980s, although 40 per cent of the black community was born in Britain and those born outside had been in Britain for at least 30 years, the media continued to treat black people as outsiders. Racist reporting in the national tabloids intensified. Tabloid papers competed to see which could be the most outrageous in their attack upon the black community. The opportunity was seized when violence broke out between young mainly African-Caribbean males and police in 1981 and again in 1985. The media used these 'uprisings' to attack Britain's black population.

The 1981 violence in Handsworth and Brixton was presented by the majority of newspapers as lawless African-Caribbeans attacking the police and looting shops. '150 Black Youths Clash With Police' said *The Daily Mail* (11/4/81). *The Sun* painted an image of war in its headlines 'Battle of Brixton' and went on to reaffirm the racist view that 'Brixton, the heart of the West Indian Community, is notorious for muggings, assaults and murders' (11/4/1981). When the 1985 disturbances broke, neither the government nor the media had learnt anything from what happened in 1981. All African-Caribbeans were branded law-breakers – not just those involved in the violence. Yet the media still failed to highlight the social and economic problems of Britain's black community. Bias and insensitive reporting continued but this time the media, especially newspapers, portrayed the violence as a result not of racism but of inter-racial conflict. It was African-Caribbeans against whites and Asians. The colonists' divide and rule policy was put into play.

The death of a police officer, Keith Blakelock, during the 1985 disturbances made matters worse and newspaper reports began to read more like fiction. Some blamed the uprising on communists, from both inside and outside the United Kingdom, asserting that street-fighting experts had been trained in Moscow and Libya. *The Daily Mail* warned the black community that if it continued with what the paper saw as 'Murderous Assaults', white society would launch a 'paramilitary reaction unknown to mainland Britain' (8/10/85). However, there was no mention of the continuing assaults on or racism against black people.

Campaigning against media racism

Despite blatant racism common in Britain's media, by the 1980s hundreds of Black Britons were choosing journalism as a career and hoping to put the records straight. But the media, especially newspapers, accepted only a few – for most the doors to mainstream journalism remain closed. Many potential black journalists had to give up their ambition of becoming journalists or go to work in the black press. This situation led to the first black media campaigning organisation in Britain in 1981, the Black Media Workers' Association (BMWA).

The BMWA's inaugural meeting was attended by over one hundred black people working in different sectors of the media, such as films, video, public relations, advertising and journalism. They came together to campaign for better representation in media training, jobs and the portrayal of black people. So important was this organisation that memberships rose in the first year to 1,000, demonstrating the extent to which black people wanted to be a part of the media.

The BMWA was founded at a time when the left of British politics was aware of racism and the power of the media to influence race relations. The BMWA timing was right and the organisation was able to get funding from media unions, such as the NUJ and ACTT, but the biggest financial support came from the GLC Ethnic Minorities Unit. The GLC had rightly taken an anti-racist stance and had to put its money where its mouth was.

Yet the BMWA lasted only five years and did not manage to fulfil most of its aims. The main reason for its failure was that by 1985 most of those active in the organisation had left for jobs in *Channel 4* and other parts of the white media. In addition, its main funder, the GLC, was abolished. Sivanandan explained the demise of the BMWA in critical terms:

> The fall came after the white media made room for them in ethnic slots. Since then they have gone back to being either Afro-Caribbeans or Asians. None of these gave a fart for ordinary black people but use them and their struggles as cynically as any other bourgeois class or sub-class. The BMWA in the short period of its fight to get into *Channel 4* never did anything for the lower ranks of black workers. (1988, 40)

As a member of the BMWA from 1982 until its demise in 1987, I agree broadly with Sivanandan's criticism because, while many members of the organisation were genuinely interested in campaigning against racism, a significant number wanted only to secure jobs for themselves. The new Channel 4 was an obvious target because it was set up in 1989 to help redress the balance in broadcasting by providing, amongst other things, ethnic minority programmes. Ambitious and single-minded black journalists, many of them members of the BMWA's General Committee, were competing for jobs on the new station. Many had talks with white media employers which should have been about the organisation but were more about making deals for themselves. The BMWA did however manage to carry out the first research study into black media workers in 1983 and also compiled a black media workers' directory.

Another organisation, the Black Journalists' Association (BJA), was set up in 1988 but closed five years later. Unlike the BMWA, it had very few aims; some said none at all. In principle it was committed to better representation of black people in journalism training and jobs but in practice it did little to achieve this. The organisation was no more than a social gathering of journalists and other media workers. I attended nearly all its meetings and found it a useful place to catch up with gossip and meet journalists I had lost contact with. But few people took the organisation seriously as part of a campaign for equality in the media. Mainly, the organisation was not run by an elected body but by its three male founders who worked as full-time journalists and who eventually did not have the time to run the organisation. Like the BMWA before it, the Black Journalists' Association had to close because its organisers could not, or did not want to, combine full-time employment in the media with campaigning activities. Very few black journalists want to get involved in anti-racist activities. One organiser of the BJA told me: 'We tried to get other people to take over when we found we did not have the time to carry on but no one came forward'.

Campaigning from inside

The experiences of the BMWA and the BJA highlight the difficulties black journalists' organisations have with campaigning for equality. The truth is that a good many black journalists, although they want equality, are not prepared to put in the time and effort needed for change. Yet they accept the benefit from the work of those who do put their careers at risk to campaign for equality. Some black journalists are committed to anti-racist organisations until they find a job – and then suddenly their commitment is to themselves only.

Black journalists who are politically aware and wish to get involved in anti-racist campaigns have to make a difficult choice between their journalistic career and 'the cause'. A television journalist who was faced with such a choice told me:

> I believe in the principle of getting more blacks in the media, but I can't get involved with these organisations because I will lose my job and if I do who is going to pay my rent? None of these groups can help me and I have to live.

This attitude was typical of over 90 per cent of the journalists I interviewed, which shows that black journalists are no different from white journalists in the pursuit of job and career advancement. And who can blame them for wanting to look after their own interests? The problem is that they are not insured against racism just because they have jobs in the white media. Employers don't discriminate against white journalists because of their skin colour. Black journalists must remember that equality, especially for black people, is not given freely and has to be worked for.

Black journalists who put the principle of equality above career are doubly discriminated against and most are unable to find staff jobs in the mainstream media. These journalists have to settle for relatively lesser jobs in left-wing publications, or work as information officers in Labour-run local authorities. Many black journalist activists have to turn to freelance work because media employers will not give them staff jobs because of their political activities. As a result, many are relatively low-paid with not much prospect of career development. However, the work of the conscious and committed black journalist is essential if there is to be a change which benefits everyone and especially future black journalists. As Kofi Hadjor, former-editor of *Third World Book Review*, explained:

> The job of a committed black journalist is to serve the black community, not the other way round. For committed black journalists there is no such thing as the 'objective', 'impartial' viewpoint. They should start from the assumption that the establishment press propagates establishment views and it is their duty to propagate the views of the people, first and foremost, black people, but also the working masses at large... Committed black journalism to be worthy of its name should seek out and expose every instance of oppression, every example of injustice against black people.' (1986, 17-18)

Making a difference

Many injustices are being challenged by many black journalists working in the white media. Although these journalists may not be active in anti-racist campaigns, they are able to bring about change even if at a modest level. An Asian journalist working on a local newspaper explained how her presence in the paper made a difference:

> None of the journalists here had ever seen or worked with a black journalist before I came here. It was uncomfortable at first but they soon got used to me when they realised that, although I was black, I was human like them. After about a month, a white reporter showed me a story he had written about an Asian family. He had spelt the

names wrong and had said the family came from India when they came from Pakistan. This reporter did not know that there was a difference between India and Pakistan. I had to put him straight. He accepted gladly what I said and after that my opinion was always asked when they were considering writing a story about Asians or their culture.

This woman found she was able to educate other journalists on the paper regarding Asian people and their culture. One white reporter wanted to know how she was allowed out of the home to train and work as a journalist, because he thought that Asian women had arranged marriages and weren't allowed to work. Her very presence at the paper made white reporters begin to question their stereotyped views of black people.

The greater employment of black people is the key to eradicating the white media values which make a nonsense of the claim that Britain is a multi-racial multicultural society.

Conclusion

This chapter has shown how racism in society, and particularly the media, has helped to prevent all but a few black people from taking up journalism as a career. The media not only reflects the structural racism in society but helps to maintain it. During the 1960s and 1970s, black journalists on national papers and television were rare. Although this is less true of the 1990s, there are still disproportionarely few and the campaign for better representation of black people in the white media has to go on. But what of those black people who were able to get into journalism? The following chapters examine their experiences.

CHAPTER 2

BLACK JOURNALISTS AND EDUCATION

Race and education since the 1960s

Since the 1960s most reports on race and education (for example, Rampton, 1981, Swann, 1985 and OFSTED, 1996) have found that pupils of African-Caribbean descent under-achieve in state schools. Black pupils' inferior culture, family life, intellect and lack of identity is still believed by some to be the reason, although such genetic theory is officially discounted. This argument was used by writers such as Eysenck in Britain and Jensen in America. Eysenck wrote:

> all evidence up to date... suggests the strong and indeed overwhelming importance of genetic factors in producing the great variety of intellectual differences which we observe in our culture and much of the difference between certain racial groups. (1971, 126)

This view also has adherents outside education. *The Bell Curve* (1994) by Richard Herrnstein and Charles Murray, two American sociologists, maintains that America's racial hierarchy, in which whites take the top jobs and earn the most money while blacks are over-represented in low-paid, low status jobs and in welfare, reflect the genetic superiority of whites.

During the 1960s, the government gave support less to genetic explanations and more to notions of the inferiority of the cultures and family patterns of immigrant children. The Department of Education and Science Circular 7/65 brought in the contentious programme of 'bussing' in 1965 in an effort to disperse the 'problem' of black pupils and prevent schools from becoming predominantly black. In circular 8/65, the government explained its position:

It will be helpful if parents of non-immigrant children can see that practical measures have been taken to deal with the problems in the school and that the progress of their own children is not being restricted by the undue pre-occupation of the teaching staff with the linguistic and other difficulties of immigrant children (DES, 1965, 2).

It was the viewpoint that black culture and language were inherently inferior that evoked the integration and assimilation periods in race and education. If black immigrants took on the British way of life they would become more acceptable and the race problems in schools, if not in society, would disappear. But these strategies failed because the problem was not with black pupils or their culture but with racism in schools and society..

Educational research
Educational research in the 1960s saw black pupils as problems and not on how racism affects these pupils' education. Researchers such as Houghton (1966) set out to gather evidence to prove the theory that children of West Indian descent were intellectually inferior. When such studies failed to back up the genetic theory, writers such as Coleman and Moynihan (1965) and Rainwater and Yancey (1967) turned to the theory of cultural and social inadequacy to explain black underachievement, blaming black families and especially black mothers. They compared Asians' educational performance with West Indians' on the mistaken basis that all Asian children succeed and all West Indian children fail.

It was not until 1971 when Bernard Coard, then teaching in London, published his book *How The West Indian Child is made Educationally Subnormal in the British Educational System* that the dreaded word 'racism' entered the debate on race and education. Coard's book responded to the concerns of the West Indian Community at the number of their children being placed in educationally sub-normal (ESN) schools. Coard described the process of the self-fulfilling prophecy and for the first time teachers were implicated in the under-achievement of black pupils. Coard argued that white teachers, as part of a racist society, had low expectations of black pupils and so under-estimated their abilities:

Most teachers absorb the brainwashing that everybody else in society has absorbed, that black people are inferior and less intelligent than white people. Therefore the black child is expected to do less well in school.

Coard maintained that:

> The black child labours under three crucial handicaps: low expectations on his part about his likely performance in a white controlled system of education; low motivation to succeed academically because he feels the cards are stacked against him; and finally low teacher expectations which affects the amount of effort expended on his behalf by the teacher and affects his image of himself and his abilities. If the system is rigged against you and if everyone expects you to fail, the chances are you will. (Coard, 1971, 25)

Coard's findings brought denial from white educationalists but West Indian parents were not surprised; they already knew that racism was the problem. After 25 years not much has changed: the Ofsted report (1996) found that many children of African-Caribbean descent, especially boys, were still failing in British state schools and that low teacher expectations about these children's academic ability is partly to blame. What is more, African-Caribbean pupils are more likely to be excluded from school than any other group.

Lip service is given to equal opportunities in education but little is done to change the system and so racism is still a fact in many schools. The National Curriculum is still Eurocentric and teacher training rarely includes anti-racist education. The result of inaction is that another generation of African-Caribbean pupils leave school without qualifications or hope.

Although six per cent of Britain's population is not white, black teachers are still the exception in British schools. Many more black teachers are needed, especially African-Caribbeans. They are vital as role models for black pupils' confidence and they show white pupils that black people are quite capable of being teachers. However, black graduates are not encouraged to take up teaching because of the glass ceiling imposed by racism.

A keynote speaker at a NUT Black Members' Conference told *The Voice*:

> Lack of career progression has long been a problem amongst black teachers. Too many workers have seen themselves work for years, but every time a place on a management course comes up it tends to be white teachers who get sent along. As a result, white teachers are at the top of the queue in being promoted to senior positions. (*The Voice*, August 1995)

My educational history

As an African-Caribbean journalist, my own educational history is an appropriate background to a discussion about the educational experiences of black journalists.

I was born in Jamaica and spent the first 12 years of my life there. My first educational experience was with four other children in the sitting room of my day-minder, who was a retired teacher. My grandmother paid one shilling per week to keep me there – an expense for my family who were desperately poor. Despite my poverty I was not treated differently from the other children. In fact, once my minder found I was keen to learn I was treated rather better. I remember her teaching me to write and gently guiding my hand. I spent two wonderful years with her and when I left to go to school I could read and write well and was addicted to books.

The primary school I went to was poorly equipped, as many state schools in Jamaica were then and still are. There were few books and over thirty children in the classes – but there was no racism. Apart from one or two Asians, all the children were black Jamaicans and so were the teachers. I remember looking at my teacher and thinking that one day I would like to do her job. It never entered my thoughts that I might not be able to do so because I was poor. By the age of ten I plucked up enough courage to ask my teacher what I needed to do her job. She smiled and said, 'I like pupils with ambition'. Then she set about telling me what I had to do and it seemed out of my reach. Although I was confident that I could pass the required examinations I saw no hope of getting into teacher training college because my family could never afford the fees. However, my addiction to books continued and the more I read the more I wanted to know. I generally had no problems with homework but when I did teachers always helped.

Both my primary and secondary schools in Jamaica were strict. Our uniforms had to be clean and neat, even if they were not new. They were regularly inspected and if they were not up to standard we were sent home. There were strict rules on how pupils should behave in schools and towards teachers and caning was customary. In extreme cases, pupils would be expelled but this rarely happened because expulsion from school was seen by a wider community as a disgrace to the pupil and their family.

Despite the poverty of the school and its pupils, we were all encouraged to do the best we could academically. Education was considered the greatest asset a person could have, second to money. At eleven I passed a scholarship for a private girls' school but although my parents did not have to pay fees, they could not afford to pay for uniform, food and all the other expenses. I was very disappointed but I still believed that I could pass my exams and become a teacher.

I came to England a year later and everything changed. For the first year I was one of only three black pupils in my secondary school. I was called names like 'monkey' and asked why I didn't 'go back to the jungle?' Some pupils even asked me if I had a tail. One day I showed them that in fact I didn't have a tail that I was no different from them. In the end, I was fed up and I punched a girl who was calling me names and ended up with a warning.

Teachers didn't take any notice of me and I didn't care. But I did care when they put me in a remedial class because they said they couldn't understand my Jamaican accent. I could read better than anyone in the remedial class and do better maths. Eventually, I was put back into mainstream class. It was then that I decided that, even if I couldn't become a teacher, I needed to prove to the teachers who acted as if I were invisible that I was not stupid. Despite my hard work, teachers saw fit to enter me for CSE instead of GCE. I said nothing because there was no point; I was a poor, powerless, black child. I took and passed six CSEs at grade one, which was equivalent to GCE but that did not matter as they were still only CSEs and I wanted GCEs. I could not wait to leave secondary school and as soon as I did I enrolled in night class and took eight GCEs in one year, atttaining grades A-C. It was one of the proudest days of my life. I went to work full-time and some years later returned to education as a mature student. I did three 'A'-levels, then a degree in English language and literature.

I was the only one of my black contemporaries who managed to succeed academically and attend university. The others left school with very little education. Many of the girls had babies and resigned themselves to life on the dole. Many of the men didn't fare much better, finding menial jobs if they were lucky. When I went to university, the people I had known at school stopped speaking to me. They saw me as a sell-out because I wanted to succeed in the 'white man's world'. But I didn't lose any sleep over this because I wanted to succeed despite racism. By the time I entered university, I had been writing part-time for a newspaper and wanted to become a journalist.

Getting to university does not mean that I am any better than fellow African-Caribbeans who did not. My success was due partly to the sound educational grounding I received in Jamaica, which most of my contemporaries did not have. I also believe that, despite living in a racist society, education gave me confidence and choices in the job market which no amount of racism can take away.

My experience in higher education was of isolation. My first degree was in English language and literature and there was only one other black person in my group of sixty. All the lecturers were white, male and middle-class, except one white woman. I had little in common with these men but all I wanted was to get my degree, so I worked hard and achieved my dream of becoming a graduate in English.

Some years later, after training and working as a journalist, I decided to do a PhD part-time. I was the only black person aiming this high in my faculty and there were only two others in the whole university. I was rare and I was lonely. My workload was enormous as I had no idea what I had taken on. I was married with one child and working full-time. The study was expensive and time-consuming. I was offered no financial help and had to pay my university fees and travelling expenses. My research took me to different parts of the United Kingdom and Ireland, Canada and the United States.

My Ph.D took eight years. For the first two years things ran smoothly, although I had to juggle job, responsibilities at home and my study. However, at the end of my second year my supervisor left for America and it took me two years to find another. In the last three years of my study I gave up full-time journalism for freelance work which allowed me the flexibility to finish this demanding degree.

I was lucky because, although my thesis was on discrimination, neither of the two professors who supervised me asked me to change my arguments. I had much guidance on how I should present my Ph.D but not on what I should say. Walking up to the podium and accepting my doctorate was the most important day of my life. I was the only black Caribbean woman to have received this degree at the University for many years. On my way out I was approached by four African-Caribbeans who had just received their B.A. degrees. They congratulated me and said how proud they were of me because I had shown that black people can achieve if they are given the chance. Those few words made all my effort worthwhile.

Black journalists and education

Although the British education system fails many African-Caribbean pupils, some do succeed. In the past ten years a growing number of black people are entering further and higher education. Many of them left comprehensive schools without qualifications but later went back into education. Although further and higher education institutions are not colour-blind, black students generally do succeed, unlike those in comprehensive schools. In my research for this book, I found that a number of black graduates are taking up journalism. Of the 100 black journalists I interviewed, 71 per cent were graduates as compared to 55 per cent of other journalists. Some had two or more degrees, including a Ph.D. Those without degrees were all educated up to 'A'-level; only two had no educational qualifications. Black journalists have more degrees than other journalists because, as one said, 'I had to have more qualifications than whites if I was to get an equal chance'. One African-Caribbean journalist gained extra qualifications because he had 'to prove to myself and the racist society that as a black man I can succeed educationally'.

African-Caribbean journalists

To African-Caribbeans gaining high qualifications was very important because they believed that they would face more racism than Asians. To succeed in the education system meant that they and their families had to develop strategies to overcome the racism in the system.

Ten per cent of the African-Caribbean journalists I spoke to had taken the option of private education – chiefly because their parents believed that state education was racist. These journalists – apart from one – found private school a positive experience. As one said, 'I was expected to achieve, unlike in state schools where blacks are expected to fail'. Another said, 'I was never called names and picked upon by teachers'. None of these journalists objected to private education; they were proud that they had the opportunity to get their education in exclusive schools. This comment is typical: 'I only wish more black pupils were able to get private education: there would be fewer failures'.

Although most of them came from middle-class homes, this was not true of Clive, a broadcast journalist, who was adopted by a white, working-class family. His adoptive parents noticed that he was bright and set out to help and encourage him. He said that they were worried about sending him to the local comprehensive school, where they believed his love for learning would not be noticed or encouraged. Clive considered himself very lucky:

> My adoptive white parents were not rich but they encouraged me to do well at school and then gave me the opportunity to take the scholarship which I passed. I went to a top public school attended by the royals and the sons of the rich and famous. There were five other non-whites there but their fathers were either prime ministers, presidents or very rich. I was the only one there who was black and poor and that gave me a certain novelty and respect from teachers and pupils. Teachers also knew that I came there on academic merit and they expected the same from me as other pupils. There was never any limit set on what we could do academically. Because of the education I received at my private school I was able to go to Oxford where I received a first-class degree before training as a journalist. I wish more black pupils were encouraged to get a scholarship so that they can get the opportunity to get private education. It is the only way to get sure success.

Most of those I spoke to had no experience of racism in private schools, except for Brenda, a radio producer, who encountered racism from her first day at school. She was never welcomed and soon realised that the school took her only because her parents were barristers and could afford the high fees. She told me:

> I did not expect to be treated like this when my parents were paying so much money. I felt uncomfortable with some teachers and pupils. They looked at me with hate but I kept telling myself it was all in my mind but after one particular experience I knew I was right. It was during a history lesson when a teacher began explaining how Britain had civilised the 'darkies of Africa'. What was worse he and the other pupils kept looking in my direction. Instead of feeling nervous as I usually did, I told them that the only thing Britain did for Africa was to steal its wealth. Afterwards there was a deadly silence in the room. I was trembling when I sat down. I imagined being packed off home in disgrace and I awaited the order but it never came. The teacher simply turned to the blackboard and continued as if nothing had happened. I stayed on at school but was more isolated than ever.

Although private education can be an escape from racism, it is not an option for most African-Caribbean parents, who are working-class and poor. Even some middle-class African-Caribbeans find it difficult to pay the £5,000 and more per term these schools charge. Winning a scholarship is fine if you can find one but there are not many of them about and pupils have to be exceptional even to be considered.

Grammar Schools

Grammar schools were the next option for African-Caribbean parents who feared the potential racism in comprehensive schools. But like private schools, grammar schools were not open to many African-Caribbean parents. They had to compete for the limited places against white, middle-class families and were often unsuccessful, not because their children were not bright but because schools prefer white pupils. Like private schools, grammar schools have a record of high attainment, because they have more books, better facilities and smaller classes. However, some people argue that neither private or grammar schools should exist because they divide pupils. While this may be an understandable principle for white parents on the left of British politics, many black parents, especially African-Caribbeans, cannot afford to take this stance when their children are faced with a daily dose of racism in non-selective schools and are leaving without qualifications.

Separate Schools

Parents of African-Caribbean children have two other options besides comprehensive schools. One is the separate schools that have been established in Britain; the other is to send their children to the Caribbean to be educated. The idea of separate schools was part of the reaction to negative self-concepts fostered in the 1970s in the race and education debate. Black parents called for more black teachers and for the setting up of separate schools which they believed, would help West Indian children achieve.

The first such school was John Loughborough Seventh Day Adventist School, which opened in 1979 with 50 juniors and 300 secondary pupils. The £500 a term school became a show piece of educational achievement for black children. An article on the school in *The Observer* noted that:

> Rewards and incentives, structure and discipline, religious and moral education, regular tests and homework from the earliest age are all part of the mixture that has made John Loughborough a beacon of black achievement (*Observer* 21/2/88).

The school's population reflects the Seventh Day Adventist membership, so most but not all the pupils and teachers are of West Indian descent. The headteacher stresses the importance of positive role models that black teachers provide for black pupils. Jasmin Chambers, head of the junior school, said that:

> Black teachers give children someone they can identify with and aspire to... a black child is able to come to the school and not feel different or apart or awkward (*Observer, 1988*)

Two of my African-Caribbean respondents went to John Loughborough School. Vicky, a newspaper journalist, was one of the first intake at the school. She believes that her educational success was based not only on having black teachers as role models but also that the school was predicated on discipline, hard work and a Christian faith. Vicky explained:

I believe that the school helped me and others to succeed because it demanded we did a certain amount of school work and Bible study. Our Christianity was built around educational work and that gave us a firm foundation. There was never any question of failure: with God at the helm, we could succeed and many of us did.

But separate schools such as John Loughborough have been criticised by writers such as Reeves and Chevannes (1987). They argue that the school is not in the spirit of the black voluntary movement or Saturday schools, which are open to all children irrespective of educational ability or whether they can pay. They believe that John Loughborough does not lift the black community as a whole but 'only a handful of privileged black pupils at the expense of the rest of the black community' (1987, 149).

Haringey Council has always opposed the school on similar grounds to Reeves and Chevannes. In 1996 the school applied for grant-maintained status but Haringey's Director of Education opposed it on grounds that it was 'a waste of public money in a borough with huge needs for spending on primary and secondary schools' (*The Voice*, 29/11/96). The problem is that both primary and secondary schools in Haringey still fail many of their black and Caribbean pupils, whereas John Loughborough does the opposite. What separate schools like John Loughborough demonstrate, however, is that given the right atmosphere black pupils can and do achieve in education and so should not be opposed.

More than half of my African-Caribbean respondents agreed that schools such as John Loughborough and other community educational organisations were essential to help children from Caribbean descent to do well. But they saw this as a short-term answer to racism in education. A number of respondents had a more pessimistic view of the situation and wanted separate black schools because they believed that the British education system will not make the changes needed to give black children an equal chance. As one said, 'It was not in the white man's interest to change the system; they don't want to see blacks as equals.' But separate schools are not the answer to racism in education and society; surely the point is an equal and adequate system for all.

Education in the Caribbean

Some African-Caribbean journalists were sent to the Caribbean for their education. Their parents, like the parents who sent their children to private or grammar schools, think that the British education system is racist and fear that their children would not succeed in comprehensive schools. These journalists said they received more than book education in the Caribbean. They developed a strong sense of who they were and 'learnt Caribbean history and culture', which gave them a sense of belonging. They praised the discipline and hard work that the school imposed. These journalists believe that this was partly why they did well educationally. The headteacher of a school in Barbados explained:

> Our job is to keep children on the straight and narrow the attitude of children here is different; they want to succeed. (*Black Britain* BBC2, 1996)

Trevor, a broadcast journalist, told how going to the Caribbean for his education helped him.

> I was always getting into trouble, right from primary school. If anyone called me a name or just looked at me I would give them one. I didn't care what teachers thought of me. I knew they hated my black skin, so I didn't care. I was suspended many times and eventually my parents could not cope and send me to my grandparents in Barbados and my life changed. I didn't get any aggro at school any more as I did in England and teachers took a great deal of interest in pupils. The trouble was they were strict and I was not used to such discipline and it was sometimes difficult to conform but I did and it was worth it. I succeeded in school. At home I was surrounded by uncles, aunts and cousins and I learnt something from everyone about my culture. Unlike Britain, there was no colour barrier in Barbados and I saw black people as judges, lawyers, lecturers, scientists, teachers, business people and prime ministers. It gave me confidence that I could be anything I wanted to be despite my black skin. I didn't want to come back but I wanted to go to university in Britain and get a job and unfortunately there were not many jobs in Barbados at the time.

Comprehensive Schools

As we have seen, comprehensive schools fail a great number of children of African-Caribbean descent, but more than half of my African-Caribbean respondents went to comprehensive schools and most wished they had gone elsewhere. However, these journalists not only survived but left with high educational success. Gillborn (1990) argues that African-Caribbean pupils have to develop strategies if they are to succeed in schools and I found that most of my African-Caribbean respondents had managed to do so, thus managing to counter racism and low teacher expectations. They thought this 'unfair' and 'racist' and believed that the government and the Commission for Racial Equality (CRE) should be doing more to prevent racism in education and society.

Lower streams and remedial classes were the experience of many African-Caribbean respondents, despite their academic abilities. This caused anger and defiance among parents who challenged the schools about racist injustices. But many parents simply accepted the school's judgement, and others lacked the courage or confidence to do anything. Pearl, a newspaper journalist, said her mother was one of those who did challenge the school when she was demoted to a remedial class because she had a Trinidadian accent:

> When I arrived at school in London I was immediately put into a remedial class. They didn't even give me a test. They said I couldn't speak English and this was because they could not understand my accent. I was angry because the work I was given in remedial class I had already done in Trinidad. I told my mother and she presented herself at the headteacher's office. She worked as a journalist and was well-informed. She demanded that I was put back in mainstream or she would make an official report to the local education office and if she didn't get what she wanted she was going to the local paper and the CRE. I was quickly put into mainstream and they never bothered me again. But I kept my head down to avoid any more trouble.

Boys of African-Caribbean descent face an uphill struggle to get a good education in British comprehensive schools. A report by the Runnymede Trust (1996) showed that they were twice as likely to be excluded from school as others and that their educational achievement is 'very poor'.

At 16 they were far less likely than whites or Asians to enter sixth form college. Wright (1985) observed that white teachers' interaction with African-Caribbean boys 'very frequently took the form of enforcing discipline rather than encouragement or praise'.

African-Caribbean male respondents told me how they managed to achieve educationally at comprehensive schools. 'I had to keep quiet when teachers were nasty to me because if I answered back I would get into trouble.' Another said, 'If the teachers asked a question and I knew the answer I never answered for fear of bringing attention to myself.' Errol, a broadcast journalist, went even further: in order to survive his comprehensive school and get a good education, he had to be different from the other black boys, as he related:

> I didn't want to get expelled or to get in any trouble so I decided that being nice and helpful to teachers would get help and positive attention from them. I opened doors for teachers, volunteered to do work for the school, did what homework I received and asked for more. After a while two or three teachers began to notice that I was different from the other African-Caribbean boys and they helped me. The problem I had was not with teachers but with other black pupils, especially males, who called me a coconut and a sissy, which I was not. I was angry but I didn't say anything. I just kept away and did my work. If I didn't develop this strategy, I would have left school without any qualifications, like most of the other black boys in my school.

Some African-Caribbean journalists left comprehensive schools without qualifications but succeeded when they returned to further education. Desmond, a newspaper journalist, is typical:

> My comprehensive school was the pits. I was put into the lower stream and nothing was expected of me. I was never considered for GCEs. Teachers expected me to leave school and either go on the dole or go to prison but I had no intention of doing either. I wanted to become a journalist and intended to get educated. I could not wait to leave my comprehensive school. Then I enrolled at FE and did five GCEs and three 'A'-levels. I later did a degree before training to become a journalist. I think it is a disgrace how some teachers

treat black kids and get away with it. The CRE should be doing something about it.

The conflictual relationship between pupils of African-Caribbean descent and white teachers is mainly responsible for these pupils' educational under-achievement, according to (among others) Coard (1971), Driver (1977), Middleton (1983), Wright (1985), and Gillborn (1990) who have supported this view. Driver, for instance, argues that 'white teachers do not have the cultural competence' to understand the behaviour of children of West Indian descent. They misinterpret these children's behaviours as difficult and so place them in lower streams. Driver argues that: faced with the limitation of their own cultural competence, teachers often felt that the only way forward was a power-based insistence that those pupils act according to the standards which they (the teachers) stipulate for them. This tended to intensify an already conflictual situation and so to heighten the ethnic awareness of those involved (Driver, 1977, 356).

Although Britain's education system is generally racist, there are some schools which do operate effective equal opportunity policies. They do so by incorporating multicultural and anti-racist education in their curriculum and by employing black teachers who are represented in every area of the school. Sadly, these schools are too few. Multicultural and anti-racist education has never been generally welcomed by white educationists and still less by the media. Swann (1985) found that multicultural education was interpreted in different ways and this led to confusion. Stone (1981) argued that multicultural education is used to 'compensate the cultural deprivation of black, working-class children'. Anti-racist education, which exposes the historical roots of colonialism and racism, is seen as still more dangerous because it goes to the heart of the matter. It is described by the media as 'witchcraft' and an 'assault on education' and is anathema to those who want to retain the racist *status quo.*

A few African-Caribbean journalists were fortunate to go to schools which implemented equal opportunity policies and they knew that their schools were the exception rather than the rule. They had found teachers 'helpful and caring'. One told me that, 'I was encouraged to do a degree in English by my teacher when I told her that I wanted to be a journalist'.

Such schools provide anti-racist training for teachers as part of professional development and ensure that the curriculum is culturally inclusive. The result is that the respondents who attended such schools had a positive experience of education.

Sarah, a broadcaster, told me:

> Racism was never tolerated in my comprehensive school There were strict rules against it. The Local Education Authority issued anti-racist guidelines for school which meant that teachers were able to get equal opportunity training and it worked. Teachers were able to understand black culture.

Middle-class African-Caribbean parents

Parental influence and role models are important to the development of all children but doubly so to black children because of the racism in society. Many educationists have argued that middle-class children are well placed to take advantage of learning because they come to school already equipped by their middle-class background. Forty per cent of my respondents came from professional middle-class homes. This is far higher than the PSI survey of 1984, which found that only seven per cent of the African-Caribbean community were in professional occupations. Journalists and their parents belong to a growing African-Caribbean professional middle-class able to act as role models and to provide financial support and educational motivation for their children.

Some African-Caribbean journalists from middle-class backgrounds argue that racism is not the cause of black under-achievement, blaming instead single mothers who 'have several children by different men without any stable relationship with any'. They argue that these women don't take enough responsibility for their children's education and are not good role models.

Cindy, a freelance journalist, holds this view. She said:

> My education and success in my job could not have been achieved without love and encouragement from my parents: they were always there for me. I was luckier than most Caribbean children who grow up without a father: I had one there all my life and I am grateful for that. My father is a research scientist and my mother a National

Health Service manager and they expected me to achieve, which I believe is perfectly natural. They were my role models. Unfortunately most African-Caribbean children don't have any positive role models and so believe they can't be successful.

Prejudice against single mothers is not restricted to middle-class African-Caribbeans but prevails among the working-class and society in general. As we have seen, education writers in the 1960s blamed black mothers for their children's educational under-achievement whilst ignoring the racism in society. Single mothers seem to be a target for moral crusaders, black and white, who want simple answers to complex questions. The implication is that black children would succeed if only there were a man about the house – a sexist and ridiculous notion when you consider how many women and children have been abused by violent men. If children have caring parents, whether one or two, they will benefit, but this alone is not enough to overcome the racist education system which generally expects black children to fail.

Working-class, African-Caribbean parents

It is not only middle-class, African-Caribbean parents who inspire their children to get a good education. Most of my African-Caribbean sample came from working-class families and those who were brought up by single mothers did not see the absence of a father as significant in their lives. They believe 'that it's other people's problem'. They have achieved equally with African-Caribbeans from two-parent middle-class homes. With just one proviso – all agreed that what was difficult was that there was not much money around. Most respondents from poor backgrounds said that they were determined to do well because they did not want to end up in low-paid jobs like their parents. A broadcast journalist recalled:

I was one of five children but I was the brightest and my parents, though uneducated, recognised this. They took me under their wing and encouraged me, buying extra books, although most of the time they had to borrow the money. My father worked in a factory and my mother was a dressmaker. They worked so hard but never had enough money and I swore that would not happen to me.

Asian journalists and education

The educational achievement of African-Caribbeans differs from that of Asians. A report by Birmingham Education Authority (1996) showed that while African-Caribbean boys achieve below the norm in science and maths, Asians do better than pupils overall. This difference in educational success has been attributed by some educationalists and politicians to culture. Asian culture, they assert, is superior to African-Caribbean because it is based on strong moral values and encourages hard work and discipline and strong family ties. While these are admirable qualities which do help all children, thay are not the inherent qualities of 'Asian culture' alone – assuming that Asians were a homogenous cultural group. Dilip Hiro suggests that one motive for Asian educational achievement is economic.

> Outside the economic field the average Asian had no aspiration or expectations. He had come to Britain knowing full well that white people were culturally alien in his eyes and he had neither the inclination nor the intention to participate in their life (1973, 113).

But there are also other reasons for the apparent educational success of Asians compared to African-Caribbeans. Gillborn (1990) in his study of an inner city comprehensive school found that:

> In marked contrast to the myth of African-Caribbean pupils as a threat to authority, there was a general feeling among City Road teachers that Asian pupils were quiet and certainly not troublemakers. This belief survived despite the fact that teachers sometimes saw it fit to discipline Asian pupils... Classroom observation indicated that Asian pupils experienced teacher-pupil relations which were generally similar to those of their white peers of similar degrees of academic involvement (1990, 10).

Despite these differences in the educational experiences of Asians and African-Caribbeans, my research for this book found both Asian and African-Caribbean journalists to be highly educated and motivated. Asian journalists, like African-Caribbeans, said that their parents were concerned about racism and about the quality of education they would received in state schools. Twice as many Asian journalists went to private schools as African-Caribbeans, a sign of the rapidly rising Asian middle-class. Like African-Caribbeans, the experience of private schools was positive. They were treated equally with white pupils and were expected to achieved educationally. Asian journalists often regarded their private education as part of their family and social conditioning. Shiv told me:

> I was educated at the Eton of India and when I came to Britain I was sent to an exclusive public school. I did not expect my parents to send me to some inner-city state school where I would have to mix with all kinds. It would not have been socially acceptable.

However, some of my Asian respondents came from working-class backgrounds and they, like many African-Caribbeans, struggle in inner-city areas for a decent education, housing and jobs. The stereotypical view that all Asian businesses are successful is a myth. Asian journalists from small-business backgrounds talked about the hard work and long hours they and their family had to put into such businesses, without getting much out. A number told me that their parents were in business as a direct result of racism. Abdul's father, for example, was trained as a lawyer, but opened a shop because he could not find work in his profession. Many such businesses depend upon unpaid work from family members in order to make ends meet. Abdul's story is typical:

> From when I was little I had to help out in the shop which is open all day every day and half the night. I hated it but did so to help my parents. Working in the shop got difficult when I started studying for my 'O'-levels and by the time of my 'A'-levels I had to stop helping in the shop because I was too tired to study. It was either my education or the shop and I wanted to be a journalist not a shopkeeper working all hours of the day and night for a pittance.

Asian journalists and racism in state schools

Asian journalists told me that despite their educational success, they too experienced racism in their schools. Whereas African-Caribbeans were seen as 'troublemakers' they were stereotyped as 'passive Asians'. So they became targets for attacks and name-calling by white pupils who thought they would not fight back. Mohammed, a television researcher, told me:

> As an Asian I was always picked upon by white pupils while they left the black boys alone, but most of the time I gave as good as I

got. I stuck up for myself. I only ran away when there were two or three of them. When I told teachers they did not take any notice of me so I stopped trying to make them listen.

Asian journalists agreed that teachers did not expect Asian pupils to rebel, even though they occasionally did so. They also noticed that they were given more encouragement than African-Caribbean pupils but because white teachers tended to stereotype Asian pupils they expected them not to do certain subjects. Rasheed, a television journalist, said:

I told my teacher that I wanted to study English and history at university but she tried to discourage me saying that people like me should study maths instead and become an accountant or use it when I started to run a curry house.

Conclusion

The accounts by my respondents suggest that attending private schools to some extent protects African-Caribbean children and enhances their chances of achieving highly in education. On the state sector, both groups were affected by racism and for the African-Caribbean origin pupils, this meant being subjected to low expectations by their teachers.

CHAPTER 3

The professional education training
of Black journalists

Introduction

Black people are grossly under-represented in journalism courses in Britain. In the 1980s course managers claimed that this was due to black people's poor educational qualifications, or because black people simply did not apply. However, we have seen that those black people who do apply for journalism courses are in fact well-qualified. In the 1990s course selectors have a new excuse: black under-representation is now due to finance. Apparently, only middle-class whites can afford the fees for postgraduate journalism courses now that discretionary grants are almost unobtainable. The truth is that most black people don't even get an interview and so never get the chance to worry about fees. Black students, like others, can apply for and get student loans. The journalists I spoke to were willing to take out loans, if only they were accepted by colleges.

Journalism courses, if they do take on black people, take only a token few and so finance is seldom the reason for black under-representation. In 1996 the London School of Printing had two hundred students on various journalism courses, of whom ten were black (Wadsworth, 1996). Even if courses are in areas with high numbers of black people, they still take few black people or none at all. The managing director of a Midland Group of newspapers told me that in the ten years since he had been in the job he had not taken on a 'black or brown face'. When asked why, he said, 'They don't apply.'

This explanation has been rejected by black journalists I spoke to, most of whom have written dozens of application letters around Britain and who either received no reply or were rejected when they went to interview. Traditionally journalism was and still is a white, middle-class occupation.

Journalists' education

As we have seen, discrimination against black people starts with the educational system, which allows a majority to leave school without worthwhile educational qualifications. In recent years journalism has almost become a degree entry occupation, with a minimum qualification of five GCSEs grade A-Cs which and must include English language. However, this minimum is often not enough to gain entry into journalism courses. The National Council for the Training of Journalists (NCTJ) estimated that over 55 per cent of people applying for journalism courses are graduates.

The Newspaper Society declares that:

> It has always been the industry's practice to recruit graduates from any discipline and train them to become proficient journalists (1985)

This constraint unfairly affects black people, especially those of African-Caribbean descent.

Although having a degree is of advantage to journalists, as to anyone, making it the most important criterion for acceptance to courses discriminates against people who generally leave school without educational qualifications. No one really needs a degree to become a good journalist or to have specific educational qualifications, apart from being able to read and write well. I spoke to one journalist who is now a television producer, who told me,

> I left school without any GCSEs. I could read and write and that's all I wanted. What's more important is my interest in news and people. I have always been interested in what makes people tick. I got into television as a researcher and that was only because I had loads of ideas and could get the information I needed. I have never looked back.

Others in the media industry agree that having a degree is less important than having the aptitude for journalism, and they view graduates of journalism schools with suspicion. Some editors believe that journalists are born not made. Sir David English, then editor of *The Daily Mail*, thought that:

> Journalism is a skill that can only be acquired on the job and at the end of the day it depends on whether someone has a burning individual talent (1994, 342).

There is further criticism of the efforts to professionalise journalism by introducing degree entry to courses or degrees in journalism. Brian Hitchen, then editor of *The Daily Star*, stated his objections bluntly:

> I have only met one graduate from journalism school who was any good. Most of them are appalling. There is only one way to learn journalism and that's by starting at the bottom. There is a sieve in our profession that is the cruellest and the finest and only the best get to the top (1994, 345).

The NUJ Black Members' Council urged that journalistic aptitude be the main consideration when selecting applicants. Otherwise black people, working-class people, or those with modest qualifications will be ignored even though they might be capable of becoming good journalists. This does not mean that black people want to enter journalism courses with lower qualifications than whites, as we have seen, black people applying for journalism training are well educated.

Historical overview
Insistence on high educational qualifications for journalism is relatively new. Up until 1955 there was no standardised educational requirement for new recruits. The 1949 Press Commission criticised the methods of journalist recruitment and training as 'haphazard'.

It questioned newspaper proprietors about the educational qualifications of their staff and found that half of the 85 per cent who returned questionnaires said that their journalists did not complete secondary education and that only a few were university graduates. The Commission concluded that future applicants for journalism courses should be better educated.

> It is important that the journalist should have a good general education but this is not enough. He needs a fuller knowledge of history and English than his schooling will have given, a knowledge of the

processes of Central and Local governments and of the courts and at least a grounding in economics. Journalists' education needs to be higher than that of the mass of their readers and as the general level rises so should the journalists'. (1949, 30)

Although the Commission's intention was to raise the standard of journalists' education, it also indirectly discourages black and working-class people, many of whom did not have access to further education. The Commission also criticised newspapers for taking on sixteen year old recruits who only had School Certificates of Education and for catering for journalism solely by vocational training, with little regard for general education. The Commission made its view clear:

It is no doubt true that vocational training in journalism can be acquired only on the job but there is a clear distinction between learning to be a journalist and acquiring the degree of general education which it is necessary for a journalist to have. (1949-p30)

Calling for higher education gave those who wanted to make journalism into a degree-entry profession the justification to continue to raise the educational standard for journalism with the result that by the 1990s most journalists are graduates.

The elitism of journalism began in 1952, with the setting up of the National Advisory Council for the Training and Education of Junior Journalists in 1952 as a response to the findings of the 1949 Press Commission. Three years later it changed its name to the National Council for the Training of Journalists (NCTJ). The NCTJ was made up of representatives from journalists' unions, the National Union of Journalists and the Institute of Journalists, the Newspaper Society and the Guild of British Newspaper editors. Later they were joined by the Newspaper Publishers Association. In 1965 journalists' trade unions and the Newspaper Society agreed the minimum qualification for entry to journalism courses as three GCEs, one being English. By 1970 the requirements rose to five GCEs and by the 1990s, there are only a few courses which accept students with this minimum qualification.

The 1977 Press Commission

The report of 1977 Press Commission acknowledged that there had been some improvements in journalists' education and training but found them to be inadequate. The Commission agreed that the minimum qualifications be five GCEs grade A-C, to include English and two 'A'-levels (or their equivalent) but called for the encouragement of graduates into the profession. This shift led further to making journalism a white middle-class graduate occupation. However, despite its call for more graduates in journalism, the Commission was 'not persuaded that any priority should be given to establishing in this country first degree courses in journalism such as exist in the United States' (1977, 178).

The Commission identified the best qualification for journalists as a first degree in any established discipline, followed by postgraduate journalism training. This Commission, like the previous one, was understandably calling for educated journalists but it had forgotten the potential of people unable for whatever reason to gain high qualifications but able to make competent journalists. Newspapers such as *The Liverpool Echo* and *The Westminster Press* supported the view that

> There is a danger that formal education requirements may become too restrictive... the general desire to improve the intellectual quality of recruits is admirable but should not be allowed to exclude the 'natural' reporter who may be unable to pass exams (1977 Vol. 5, 29).

Despite these objections the move towards journalism becoming a graduate occupation was unstoppable. In 1991 the first graduate courses in journalism began at five colleges in the UK and those who wanted to professionalise journalism were triumphant. James Curran said that this...

> reflected a move from industrial indentureship towards higher education which will combine practical skills with analysis. This will mean that journalism training will move into the domain of higher education rather than continue on local newspapers. (*Times Educational Supplement* 31/1/92)

Curran urged that training be moved from newspapers to universities and colleges. But whereas colleges of higher education are ideal for analysing and playing with ideas, journalism is a practical occupation, like learning a trade such as carpentry or bricklaying (Tunstall, 1971). Journalists need certain practical skills best learnt on the job, whether on a newspaper, magazine, television or radio station.

Many media managers still prefer to employ journalists who have been trained or gained their experience working for local newspapers rather than those with degrees in journalism. They argue that there is insufficient theory in journalism to occupy students for three years. This is valid, since courses on journalism are padded with subjects like sociology and media history, which have little to do with writing and getting news.

The 1977 Press Commission did take a cursory look at black recruits in training and took the customary colour-blind attitude. They tried and found a reason other than racism for black under-representation on courses:

> It has been presented to us that the existing selection procedures are one cause of the lack of recruits to journalism from racial minorities though not necessarily because prejudice operates. This is an unproven and unprovable proposition and even it were true it is unlikely to be the sole explanation ... we believe that journalism is one of the occupations like teaching, the civil service and the police in which members of racial minorities should be represented as a matter of public interest. It follows that those responsible for recruitment should take positive steps to encourage members of racial minorities to come forward. (1977, 178)

The Commission's view that racial discrimination was 'unprovable' indicates that they had not read the damning surveys on racial discrimination in Britain by Daniels (1967), EJB Rose (1969) and Smith (1977) which found that racism was the norm in British society. The Commission's ignorance on the subject is astonishing. If discrimination was unprovable why was legislation needed, culminating in the Race Relations Act in 1976? It was vital that the Commission should have taken the issue of racism in the media seriously because, as we have seen, the media is not impartial on the subject of race.

On the question of sexism in journalism training and employment, the Commission was equally dismissive. They concluded that although 'very few women' were in journalism courses or had senior positions in newspapers, they would not investigate the matter because it would take an 'elaborate inquiry' and there would be 'problems' in the 'interpretations of the inquiry'. Again the Commission buried its head in the sand, refusing to accept the realities of racism and sexism not just in journalism but in society as a whole.

Traditional entry to journalism training

The traditional form of entry into journalism training is discriminatory and restrictive. Provincial newspapers, where the bulk of journalism training used to take place, recruited young white men from the local area and it helped if the prospective recruit and his parents knew the editor. It was only after the 1975 Sex Discrimination Act that journalism courses began taking on significant numbers of women and by 1997 fifty per cent of journalist students were women.

Unfortunately, journalism courses in the provinces and elsewhere did not react to the 1976 Race Relations Act in the same way as they did to the Sex Discrimination Act. Provincial newspapers have the worst record of racial inequality of any sector. Although many cover areas such as the West Midlands, Leeds, Liverpool and Cardiff, with their high and long established black populations, they train and employ virtually no black people. The only time these papers seem to take notice of the black community is when one of them is involved in crime.

Class also affects the numbers of black people taken on in journalism courses. Newspapers have always reflected the class differences in British society, resulting in polarisation between London and the provinces, between middle and working class and between the well and less well-educated (Tunstall, 1983). From their early years newspapers represented different classes of readership. Until 1855 *The Times* held a virtual monopoly in the daily newspaper field and was read by the upper class. The 'serious' papers still target a middle-class readership.

The status, salary and working conditions of provincial papers were poor but qualifications for working on them were relaxed. Christian (1980) recounts that journalists working on provincial papers before the 1950s received salaries...

comparable to that of a lower grade clerk. For both, thirty shillings or less a week was commonplace and educational qualifications for both depended on competence and literacy which the mass of the population then lacked, but neither job required much education beyond the three 'R's. Since there was no recognised union rate for either type of job ... it depended on circumstances and relations with employers. (1980, 15)

Newspapers like *The Times* and *The Guardian* have for over a century hired graduates and the breaking of the newspaper agreement in 1986 means that newspapers will continue this practice.

Boyd-Barrett (1970) noted that well over half of all journalist students came from the upper or lower middle-class. In the 1990s this is true of over 90 per cent. Editors say they want 'recruitment from a wider social and ethnic mix' (*Writing Magazine*, 1995) but they are doing nothing to achieve this. Not one undertakes ethnic monitoring. Although the black middle-class in Britain is increasing, they are still relatively few so on the class criteria only a handful of black people will be allowed into journalism training.

The fragmentation of newspaper journalism training
The NCTJ, the body which was solely responsible for newspaper journalism training, lost its monopoly in the 1980s when a number of regional and national newspapers left the NCTJ accredited scheme and set up their own. Journalism training further fragmented in 1986, when the Newspaper Society, representing provincial newspapers, failed to come to an agreement with journalists' trade unions on training. One aspect of their previous agreement was that trainees should spend three years on a provincial paper before moving on to national papers. The employers rejected this since they wished to dictate conditions of service themselves. They wanted graduates to move directly into national papers, further strengthening the graduate approach to journalism.

In 1989 the fragmentation of newspaper journalism continued and the NCTJ training system received a further setback with the establishment of National Vocational Qualifications (NVQs) and Scottish Vocational Qualifications (SVQs). In theory, NVQs should give black and working-class people without degrees more access to journalism training. NVQs can be obtained without any pre-defined entry requirements let alone a degree, whereas the NCTJ requires at least five GCSEs. Another advantage is that there is no limit to the time a candidate can take to achieve NVQs, though employers may choose to set a time limit as part of a training contract. NVQs are available at five levels, graded according to the job they relate to. Level 2 is equivalent to GCSE, level three to 'A'-levels, level four to a degree standard and level five to a postgraduate qualification. The NVQs in newspaper and periodical journalism are level four. At the time of writing, broadcast journalism has not yet taken on NVQs but it was being considered by the National Council for the Training of Broadcast Journalism (NCTBJ).

Black people and journalism training

The fragmentation of journalism training means that individual newspaper and magazine companies can and do set their own entry requirements. In fact, they can take anyone they consider suitable, as NVQs do not stipulate any educational requirements. However, my research found that not much has changed in these newspapers' methods of recruitment and so the under-representation of black people in journalism courses, especially print journalism, persists.

In its leaflet on training the Newspaper Society states that newspaper journalism:

> has a lot to offer the right person at any age for it draws on all the knowledge and skills you have ever acquired ... and leads to a tremendous sense of achievement and satisfaction. (1990, 6)

But who is considered the right person? The evidence suggests that the right person is young, white and middle-class. Black and working-class people are clearly not, because so few are accepted. Most courses do not monitor applications because they already know what kind of people they will accept. The CRE asked the NCTJ to include a question on ethnic origin with questionnaires issued to enquiries and this was done from 1986 to 1988. The NCTJ reported that only 0.04 per cent came from black people. This seemed to indicate that black people were aware that the system operated against their getting into courses and jobs. One journalist told me, 'I was afraid to apply for journalism courses because I don't see them taking many black people.'

Although the NCTJ did monitor for a limited period it did so for the CRE but not, as it announced 'for its own purposes' as information on ethnic origins 'is not a matter of concern to us' (1991). The Council did not see the matter of race equality as important. Whether this is the result of ignorance or conscious racism the effect of the Council's indifference about ethnic monitoring means that fewer black people are accepted into newspaper journalism training. Not knowing how many black people are applying for the courses they accredit gives the NCTJ an excuse to do nothing about the low numbers of black applicants. I wrote to the NCTJ in 1997 about ethnic monitoring and received no reply, which I take to mean that they still have no ethnic monitoring.

Experience with the Careers Service

Not all individuals working in the Careers Service discriminate on grounds of colour but a worrying number do. Careers officers are in a powerful position to influence the lives of young people. They are placed in a position of trust and young people of whatever colour, class or gender should be able to obtain honest and objective advice, but this is not always the case.

A report into ethnic minorities and the Careers Service found that 'ethnic minority young people have higher aspirations than their white peers', yet these aspirations were being thwarted by the 'negative evaluations' and popular stereotypes reflected in some careers officers' 'assessment of abilities and personalities' of black people (Cross *et al.*, 1990). Most black journalists I spoke to had negative experiences with the Careers Service. The following is representative of black journalists' experience with the Careers Service:

> I received no help from careers advisors about journalism. One told me to open a corner shop, because it was easy and Asians get rich from shops and restaurants. She said that my economics degree would be suitable. I was shocked that such racist people are allowed to work in the careers service.

Another journalist told me,

> When I was taking my 'A'-levels I went to a careers day at college and told the advisor that I wanted to work in radio or television as a journalist. He ignored what I had said and kept offering me advice

on bricklaying and electricianship. I told him again that I wanted to work in radio and television and this time he said that what I really want was to fix radios and televisions. With that I walked out towards the library where I found books on broadcast journalism. At least the information I got from these books was not racist.

It is evident that the Careers Service needs to put equal opportunities policies into practice. It could start by doing ethnic monitoring and then increasing the numbers of black people on its staff. Meanwhile, present staff should all have training on equal opportunities. Most importantly, there should be an effective complaints procedure to deal with racism in the service.

Higher Education is not enough

Many black journalists had hoped that having degrees would have made it easier for them to get journalism training. One said,

I did an MA because I thought it would give me a better chance. I would have done any studies which might help me to get on a journalism course, it didn't make any difference; I am black and that's what counts.

What became clear was that higher education in itself was not enough if you are black. The goalposts keeps moving so that training gets further out of the reach of most black people. Because of the limitation of accredited journalism courses in Britain – there are only eighteen in colleges and Universities – and high competition for places, entry requirements and admissions are in the hands of the course providers.

Some courses take account of where the student received their degree and whether they followed a conventional educational path, obtaining all their GCSEs at once and then moving on to A-level and university. In its 1990 report *Ethnic Minorities and The Graduate Labour Market* the CRE found that employers and courses generally dislike career and study breaks and rate former-polytechnic degrees as second-best. Many journalism courses follow this pattern, although they deny it. I found that the majority of journalism students were drawn from Oxbridge or the older universities.

Using these criteria to sift students is highly discriminatory against black people. Many leave school without qualifications and later return to further and higher education. Many get their degrees from former polytechnics. Older universities don't consider students without high grades, whereas former polytechnics will take them. I am not arguing that journalism courses should not take students from prestigious universities with excellent degrees or who have enjoyed conventional educational paths but Black and working-class people who have managed to get a degree should be recognised by course managers for their courage and determination to succeed against all odds.

Most black journalists I interviewed received their degree from former polytechnics and had not dreamed that their degree might be seen as second-best. It was because of their continued failure to get into courses that they had realised that this was partly the problem. Even those journalists who received good degrees found difficulties. One told me:

> I have a good media degree from a poly and it never occurred to me that I would find it difficult to get into journalism training. No one has told me that it is my poly degree that is the problem but I have noticed the majority of those taken on are white from Oxbridge and even the few blacks they take are also from these universities.

Although some journalism courses discriminate against black people because they have polytechnic or new university degrees, others discriminate simply on grounds of skin colour. I found black journalists who took the conventional education path and received their degrees in older universities who were also rejected. One journalist described her experience:

> I have two degrees both from London University and I applied for several journalism courses without success. It is difficult to see why I wasn't taken, apart from the fact that I am black and from a working-class background. I went to an interview for a course at the BBC and they wanted to know what school I went to and what job my parents did. I am not sure what this has to do with getting journalism training.

Ageism and journalism

Racial discrimination is not the only problem for black people applying for journalism training; ageism is another. There is no law against ageism and until quite recently it has hardly been taken seriously. Employers and trainers can and do discriminate openly against older people. As our society becomes more youth-conscious, jobs and training for those over thirty-five deteriorate and by the time people reach fifty and over they are considered useless.

According to the Newspaper Society, people of all ages can become journalists and it states that it has many hundreds of enquiries each year from people aged thirty and over. This is true in theory but in practice those over thirty find it very difficult to get training and jobs, especially if they are black. In the 1990s journalism courses still attract relatively young applicants although some aged over 25 are accepted.

The NUJ *Careers in Journalism* (1989) advised people over the age of 24 that direct entry on a local newspaper was virtually the only route. But this was not an easy route because most local newspapers did not take people over 25 as trainees because they had to pay them more and perceived them as set in their ways; younger journalists are regarded as more pliable.

Looking for training: my own experience

I was over 25 when I applied for postgraduate training in journalism. I had a good degree and had been writing news pieces and articles for college and community newspapers for several years. I had both the qualification and the commitment. I had also taught in several colleges of further education before I decided to take up journalism so I could offer a speciality. But the courses I applied for were not interested. I applied for ten courses and was invited to interview by only one. At my interview I was told that if they took me I would be the oldest person on the course and that it was highly unlikely that I would be taken on by a newspaper afterwards. They advised me to seek training in magazines which they thought would better suit my age.

However, I was determined not to let racism, sexism, or ageism stand in my way. I began to look at alternative ways of getting training and I knew then, as now, that journalism is a craft that did not have to be learned in a college or university. I heard that a local paper in the East End of London was looking for volunteers to write and presented myself in the editor's office feeling very nervous. I needn't have worried, as I was welcomed. I offered to work three days a week if the paper would give me training and they did. At first I went around with experienced journalists who showed me what to do. I learnt how to write news stories, feature writing and subbing. I stayed at the paper for two years and it published all the stories and features I wrote. I also worked with several other black people on a section of the paper which was used for black community news called *The Voice*. One of the people helping was the man who later started the *Voice* newspaper, Val McCalla. I spent two years on the paper and left for a full-time job in journalism.

Although the conventional way into journalism training, especially newspapers, is all but closed to the over 30s, there are alterative ways of getting training – and you don't need a degree either. All that is necessary is determination, journalistic aptitude and a love of hard work.

A black radio producer told me how she got into journalism at 37. She gave up her previous job as an accountant because she had always wanted to work in radio.

I wrote dozens of letters begging them to give me training, I must have written to every radio station in England. I was prepared to work for nothing just to learn the ropes, but most said that they didn't train people. Others simply did not reply. I could not get into a radio postgraduate training because I did not have a degree and I was too old. Eventually I heard that the local hospital radio station was looking for people to help out. They accepted me and I was taught how to interview and edit tapes. Eighteen months later I found a job in the BBC doing an ethnic slot. At first it was only one hour a week but this led to other jobs. I am now producing.

Applying for mainstream courses
For most black journalists, applying for mainstream courses and being regularly rejected when they have the qualifications and aptitude, is discouraging. Even more distressing is the raising and dashing of their hopes. A number told me how they were called for interviews because they had English names. They were filled with hope until they presented

themselves. Once their colour was apparent, they were rejected outright. One newspaper journalist described what happens:

> I went to an interview at a college and I had all the education they were looking for. I carried a portfolio of all the published writings I had done but as soon as they saw me, you should have seen the surprise on their faces. They thought I was white because I had a Scottish name. I was doomed from that moment because it was obvious they did not want a black person on the course and I was not taken. No reason was given, only that my application was unsuccessful. The course did not have one black person on it.

Other journalists who had been called for interviews found that interviewers were not interested in what they could offer. Applicants were asked about their politics, especially on the so-called 'Third world'; what school they went to and what jobs their parents did. One journalist was asked what country he came from, although his application stated that he was born in London. He told me:

> I could not believe that people who are responsible for journalism training could have been so ignorant. They did not even bother to look closely at my application, neither did they notice that I had a London accent. They did not take me but I was not surprised.

Black journalists told me that they were very angry about being turned down for training when they had the requisite educational qualifications. Many had taken postgraduate courses in order to improve their chances but this did not help. What was worse, they were never told why they were turned down. If a debriefing were obligatory, it might make it more difficult for course selectors to discriminate. The general view of most black journalists I interviewed is captured by one:

> Blacks are not given the same opportunities as whites by journalism courses. They do this because they know that if you haven't got the training you can't get certain jobs. This is a way of keeping black people out and keeping the media white.

What journalism courses say about recruitment

When asked about low intake of black people the selectors' replies shifted over the decades. In the 1980s they claimed that black people just did not apply or that they did not have the required educational qualifications. The Black Media Workers' Association (BMWA) of 1983 survey stated:

The common arguments that black people do not come forward and do not have the necessary qualifications have been brought into question by the overwhelming response to the BMWA courses. The reason for the under-representation of blacks on established courses must be that those institutions are not making their courses accessible to black people by failing to make contact through careers officers and schools and advertisement.

As we have seen, there are a number of well qualified black people wanting journalism training but who have been rejected. The controller of Management Development at BBC television, Robert Rowland told a black conference on the media in 1989 that the black-only reporters course at the BBC set up in 1988 was over-subscribed. The BBC advertised the course in the national and ethnic press and received 900 applications for six places. He reported that:

We did preliminary interviews with 98 people. The standard was extremely high and the six who were selected succeeded in a highly competitive situation (1989, 33).

The numbers of black people in Britain's 18 universities and colleges which do accredited journalism courses remain low. For example, in 1996 the London College of Printing had 200 students of whom 10 were black. The Director of Studies in the School of Journalism said that 'We are based in London, which has a large black population, but we have a disappointingly low number of black students. Very few present themselves for interview' (Wadsworth, 1996). But how can they present themselves for interview if they are not asked? The director did not say whether he monitored applicants. Nor did he say what he was doing to attract black people to the courses.

The problem is that course managers say they take a 'colour blind' attitude to students but it is evident that they do not. Course directors who want to change and give non-whites equal access to journalism training must monitor applicants and take action to improve the numbers of black journalist students. They must advertise these courses in the national and the ethnic press, stating that they welcome black applicants. There are decades of discouragement to be overcome.

Getting on courses

City University has for many years made sure that up to ten per cent of its intake are black. They also employ black lecturers in journalism, something which is rarely done. City University and the University of Wales, Cardiff are the only two centres which have postgraduate journalism courses which cater for black overseas students. Most other courses take on only a token few black people.

Black journalists who were admitted to mainstream courses found that they were alone on the course or that there were only one or two others out of hundreds of students. There appears to be an unstated law that only a token few black people be accepted for journalism training. Once this quota is filled it does not matter how good the next black applicant is. Black people getting onto a mainstream journalism course depends on luck. If they apply to the right course at the right time to make the quota, they have a chance.

A television journalist told me that he was accepted on his course during the 1980s because the CRE had criticised the course the year before for not having any black students:

> I was told by my tutor that I was accepted because the college want to show that it had no prejudice against non-whites. The fact that I am a graduate with lots of writing experience when I applied for the course did not seem to be important.

However, there are others who resent the idea that they were taken on mainstream courses because of luck or as the token black. They argue that: 'I was accepted because I was good and had the ability to train as a journalist', 'Being black had nothing to do with anything. I was taken on because I never gave up. I was determined to get on a good course and I did'. 'I had the right qualification and I proved at my interview that I could do the course and make a good journalist. That was the only reason why I was taken on.'

All the black journalists I interviewed had the qualifications and ability to train as journalists if given a chance but out of a hundred only 20 were accepted into mainstream journalism courses while another 25 found places on black-only courses. The other 55 per cent learnt journalism skills either on the job or through short evening or correspondent courses.

Black-only journalism courses

Due to the gross under-representation of black people on mainstream journalism courses, several black-only courses were set up in the 1980s, in response to pressure from the CRE and black journalist groups such as the NUJ Race Relations Working Party (RRWP), and the general anti-racist campaign going on at the time. The BBC was particularly criticised because of its white middle-class image and the fact that, as a public broadcasting organisation, it was taking money from black people through licenses yet employing and training so few black people as journalists.

Black-only courses were allowed under the 1976 Race Relations Act and seen as positive action. The Act allowed training bodies such as the Manpower Services Commission and the Industrial Training Boards to provide positive action training when...

> within the previous 12 months there were no members of a particular racial group engaged in particular work in Great Britain or that the portion of persons of that racial group among those engaged in such work was small in comparison with the proportions in Great Britain. (1976, para 7.8-7.9)

In the early 1980s the Manpower Services Commission (MSC), together with the CRE, began the first black-only journalism course at the Polytechnic of Central London (now Westminster University) and later the BBC set up several black-only courses. The courses attracted large numbers of applicants, most of whom had been turned down by white mainstream courses. Those who applied did so because they did not have to compete with whites.

The Polytechnic of Central London (PCL) course was set up in 1983, starting with a pilot course for 20 students, ten in radio and ten in print. The course was funded by the MSC and its objective was to achieve credibility with potential employers and be judged fit for accreditation by bodies such as the NCTJ and the Joint Committee for the Training of Radio Journalists. The course should also meet the special needs and aspirations of black student journalists.

The bulk of the PCL course concentrated on basic reporting, news writing, information gathering, interviewing, production skills, law, local government, shorthand and typing. But it also paid close attention to the issue of racism in the newsroom and in reporting practices and covered the development of the black press and broadcasting. There were 150 applicants for the first PCL course but only 20 places, for which 75 were shortlisted. The numbers of black people who applied for these courses brings into question the view that black people don't apply to be journalists.

The print journalism course ceased after one year. It had accepted students from a wide range of ages and educational ability and some could not cope with the demands of the course. Later it was decided that that students over the age of thirty would have difficulties getting newspaper jobs because of ageism in the industry. The final blow came when, because of these problems, the NCTJ refuse to accredit the course. But the radio journalists course continued and has trained some 200 black people who have mostly found full-time jobs in the media.

The same institution, now Westminster University, obtained funding in 1990 for a black-only periodical journalism course, the first of its kind in Britain. Its aims are:

> To provide for members of ethnic minorities a comprehensive training in the basics of magazine and periodical journalism, conforming to the accepted professional practice and the latest guidance of the Periodical Training Council (PTC). To equip students with greater self-confidence in overcoming any barriers that exist in the path of ethnic minorities to careers as professional journalists...

> In addition the course team hopes to strengthen the independent ethnic media by providing a focus for training, professional advice and discussion, drawing on the experience, skill and resource of minority communities, media and voluntary agencies. (Tullock, 1991, 1)

Like the radio journalism course, applicants to the periodical course did not at first have to be graduates. Emphasis was placed on aptitude, but even so over 50 per cent of the initial applicants were graduates, so the college upgraded both the radio and periodical courses to postgraduate diplomas. Course organiser John Tullock said that, 'There is an increasing number of black graduates who need training and the media industry is going mostly for graduates.' This is another example of how journalism is becoming a graduate-only profession. It is especially unfortunate when a black-only course closes its doors to black people without degrees when so many black people, as we have seen, leave school without worthwhile qualifications.

Unlike Westminster University's black-only courses, Vauxhall College in South London's black-only radio and print journalism courses do take non-graduates. They began in 1987 as an access course for black people without educational qualifications. After completing the course many students applied for and were accepted into pre-entry journalism courses which at the time took non-graduates. In 1992 Vauxhall College began a pre-entry newspaper journalism course for black people, the first since the one at PCL was abandoned in 1984. The course is recognised by the NCTJ. It takes in 20-30 trainees each year. Most of its students get into local newspapers and then take their newspaper proficiency test. The development of these course indicates a positive attitude to equal opportunities in the media and has helped to increase the numbers of black journalists since 1984. However, most journalism courses, including black-only ones are moving towards graduate entry.

In 1988 the BBC began running three courses to provide training for black people in television and radio. The Asian and African-Caribbean Reporters Training Trust provided eight bursaries of 16 months duration for training in basic television reporting. This runs in conjunction with the BBC World Service and provides training to black people as radio reporters. The BBC also runs a Television Production Trust which provides eight bursaries for black trainees to follow television production training.

Nevertheless, the BBC was and still is a white middle-class establishment and it still takes very few black or working class people on journalism courses and jobs. Anti-racist groups complained and campaigned against the racial inequality in the BBC and the company responded with these courses but this in turn angered right-wing politicians who saw separate training as reverse racism. In an effort to please everyone, the BBC gave in to its critics on separate training by closing all its black-only courses in 1994, while vowing that it would increase the numbers of black trainees in its mainstream courses. But I fear the BBC will go back to its old ways of exclusion or tokenism, like the rest. It is up to black people and particularly black journalists, with the help of the CRE, to make sure that the BBC has a fair representation of black people on its training courses and in jobs and that the company honours its equal opportunity commitments.

Reaction to black-only courses

Although black-only journalism courses are a positive way of redressing the balance in journalism training, the majority of black journalists I spoke to disapproved of them. Not because of the course content, but because some saw them as 'apartheid'. Most respondents prefer mixed courses, arguing that separate courses were not in the long-term interest of black journalists. The following illustrate the feeling of many black journalists to separate training:

> There are two arguments to these courses. One is that mainstream courses should take on more black people. The second is how employers see these courses. I am sure they see these courses as inferior and people who train on them will not get very far.

Another said:

> These courses are run by white liberals for blacks. It's like colonisation. These courses do not answer the problem of racism and the need for more black people being admitted into mainstream journalism courses. All they do is to let places like the BBC off the hook so they don't need to accept more black people onto their mainstream courses.

While I agree that separate courses are not ideal and will not benefit black journalists in the long term, what cannot be ignored is that in the short term they have helped hundreds of black people to get training. Black-only courses are in no way inferior to mainstream courses: they are accredited by the industry's appropriate body and future employers should be aware that this is the case. In an equal and just society, separate courses would not be needed.

Some of the journalists agree with me. One journalist said:

I think these courses are a good idea. They redress the historical imbalance while improving chances for black people.

Another said:

I was a student on one of these courses and it was the only way I could have got journalism training after trying several times to get into mainstream courses. They give black people a black perspective by including the history of slavery and colonisation.

Sponsorship

Sponsorship is particularly helpful for mature students who might not get student loans and are unable to fund themselves. A number of media organisation have sponsored a small number of black people to train as journalists, including *The Guardian*, Channel 4 and LWT. Black people who are fortunate enough to obtain sponsorship treasure the opportunity. One respondent who was sponsored by *The Guardian* told me:

I wrote to *The Guardian* as soon as I was guaranteed a place on a post-graduate course and I was funded. I was very lucky because at the time I was 35 and older than other trainees. I don't know why I was chosen. Maybe it was because I am a woman, or maybe my application letter was more impressive than anyone else's. But it doesn't matter why; the main thing was I was able to do the course. I would have had to give up the course if I wasn't funded and I would never have been able to work as a journalist. I will be a *Guardian* reader for life!

The NUJ was the first Trade Union to offer sponsorship to black people when it set up the George Viner Memorial fund in 1987. The Fund was never short of well qualified applicants and it has so far given financial assistance to over 100 people. The Fund is very important to me because it was my idea. I joined the NUJ in 1984 and after an active year in the Union I realised that equality in the Union was only a paper policy and practical action was needed.

In 1986 I came up with the idea that the NUJ should at least sponsor one black person each year on a recognised journalism training course. My colleagues in the former Race Relations Working Party (RRWP) supported my proposal and I took it to the Union's Annual Delegate Meeting in 1986, where I had to speak on it. I was nervous as I had never spoken in public before and certainly never to 500 journalists. I managed to persuade them that sponsorship of black people on journalism courses was essential if the Union wanted to see more black people in journalism. I pointed out that among the 500 journalists at conference only four of us were black – a clear indictment of recruitment practice. Conference agreed to my proposal and The George Viner Memorial fund was born. A recent applicant wrote to the Fund,

I am one of the successful applicants for the George Viner Fund. I successfully completed the Postgraduate Diploma in Periodical Journalism and was fortunate enough to find an internship quite soon after completing the course for a financial news wire service. After six months I was offered a full-time job. I am a press summary reporter. I would like to thank those at the George Viner Fund for the opportunity in being able to complete my course. It has opened a whole new world for me. I have met people and have been presented with other opportunities I would not ordinarily have had.

CHAPTER 4
BLACK EMPLOYMENT IN THE BRITISH MEDIA

Introduction

Black journalists find it four times more difficult to get jobs than white journalists because of colour discrimination, whether direct or indirect. The media has perpetuated negative images of black people while virtually ignoring racism. Black people who want to become journalists are discouraged by racist careers officers and journalism training schools but even when they overcome these difficulties they face yet more discrimination when they seek a job in the mainstream media.

Provincial newspapers

Provincial newspapers, as we have seen, are the traditional training ground for journalism. Although in the 1990s there exists a number of pre-entry newspaper journalism courses in colleges of further and higher education, students who complete their courses are still expected to gain experience in local and provincial papers before going on to national papers.

Provincial newspapers have a dismal record for hiring and training black journalists. Only fifteen out of 8,000 journalists working in local or provincial papers are black. In areas such as the West Midlands, where thousands of black immigrants have settled since the 1960s, most papers do not have a single black journalist. The Black Media Workers' Association (BMWA) survey in 1983 found only six black journalists in Britain's provincial papers and I suppose we should be grateful that the numbers have risen but an increase of eight over fourteen years is nothing to shout about. If black people were proportionally represented in journalism, there would need to be seven or eight hundred.

The editors and managers of provincial papers say they take a colour-blind attitude to applications for training and jobs and will employ anyone they consider suitable for the job. However, this argument obviously indicates that black people are not considered suitable. Notions of suitability are highly subjective and the conscious or unconscious desire is to keep their staff white, since the fact is that many black people have applied to them for training and jobs.

Managers of most provincial newspapers whom I spoke to have no intention of changing their employment practices. None did ethnic monitoring, a basic equal opportunities requirement, and none saw the need for it. They deny that there is a colour problem in the media or in British society.

Traditionally, local and provincial papers employ the sons and daughters of the community, preferably those they know. Because the black presence has been ignored by these papers on every level except for reporting crimes in which they are involved, it is not surprising that black people are ceasing to apply for journalism training and jobs on these papers. Those courageous enough to apply are turned down. But the papers should be obliged to represent the whole community they serve, and the most effective way to do this is to train and employ black journalists in proportion to their numbers in the community.

The editor of one Liverpool newspaper with a large black readership explained to me why he did not have a single black journalist on his paper:

> I would like to have more black and Asian staff and we have internal discussions on how this should be achieved. Unfortunately we have trained only two black journalists over the past five years and have had very few apply to us. I look forward to the day when the ethnic origins of our staff reflect society as a whole. (1994, 250)

Despite what he says about wanting to employ more non-whites he did nothing practical to change the situation. He did no monitoring and saw no need for it. Neither did he seek the advice of the CRE or the NUJ Black Members' Council about how he could find black people willing to obtain training and employment on his paper. There are hundreds of well-educated black people looking for such opportunities. But such editors clearly only pay lip-service to equal opportunities. They avoid taking action to increase the numbers of black journalists on their staff. Instead, they blame the black journalists and not their discriminatory hiring practice for black under-representation in newspapers.

One of the few black journalists who worked for this Liverpool newspaper provided an interesting insight into the real position:

> I worked for this paper for two years and left frustrated. Firstly, I was not treated like white journalists. I was a general reporter yet they wanted me to only report on 'race stories' because I am black. The editor thought that I couldn't report on white stories. In other words I was not good enough. When there was a race story I received no editorial backup. There was no paper coverage and this leads to no contact and no stories which means you are soon left with no confidence. In two years I had just three front page stories. Basically, they did not want a black reporter unless they covered black stories yet when they had black stories they did not consider them important. (1994, 259)

Other black journalists who had contacts with provincial newspapers had equally painful experiences. One journalist was called for interview and the editor could not hide his disappointment when he saw that he was black. 'He was expecting a white person because I have an English name. I didn't even get an interview. I was told after about five minutes by the editor that the job had gone.'

However, black journalists who did manage to get employment in provincial newspapers said that it was important for more black people to work on these papers. Despite the difficulties, they believed that provincial newspapers can and will change, especially if they can see that black journalists are good for business. They told me 'It can be done if more black journalists apply on spec. They should not wait for the posts to be advertised because they are not.' 'We have to prove that we are as good as them.' 'Black journalists have to market themselves to newspapers.' One black journalist who worked on a provincial paper explained how her presence on the paper altered some people's stereotyped views of black people:

When I first started working on this paper people inside and outside the office were shocked to see that a black person could write. They eventually accepted me but I was lucky. I believe that if blacks want to get jobs in these papers they have to be twice as good. Newspapers have set views and if you are different they look critically at you.

National newspapers

The numbers of black journalists employed on national newspapers are equally inadequate. At any time there are between 12 and 20 out of an average of 3,000 journalists. Every national newspaper can boast two or three black journalists and one even has a black woman sports writer. Although national newspapers take on more black journalists than provincial ones they don't take many more. One excuse used by editors and newspaper managers for the low numbers is that black journalists have no formal training. While it is accepted that national newspapers tend to employ experienced journalists, they also employ graduates with no formal training or journalistic experience.

National newspapers, like provincial papers, do not usually advertise vacancies and so black people are not able to apply and compete for jobs. Traditionally, national newspapers usually employ white, middle-class males, although since the 1975 Sex Discrimination Act more women are let in but few, as yet to senior jobs. Again there is no ethnic monitoring. When asked why they employ so few black people, editors usually respond uncomfortably. They resent the idea that the under-representation of black journalists on their paper comes down to a 'black/white issue' because, like the provincial editors they do not believe that the media have a problem with race. They also say ethnic monitoring is unnecessary because people are accepted on 'merit'.

Gordon Barkaway, director of personnel of the *Telegraph* group explained: 'We recruit and promote on merit. I believe that race and sex are immaterial – we don't support reverse discrimination.' John Honeywell, managing editor of the *Express* Group, said: 'We don't set out to exclude anybody; eventually it will happen, as more of them get on to local papers and come through, things will change' (*Independent* 25/4/1995). Another editor said he found it quite worrying that all applicants to his newspaper are white, remarking: 'I am puzzled why this is happening', but he was doing nothing to encourage black people applying for jobs.

The argument that more black journalists will be employed once they gain experience in local newspapers is a non-starter, since many of these provincial newspapers are owned by the same people who own national newspapers and they train and employ scarcely any black people.

Editors on national papers also assert that black people do not apply for jobs but they cannot prove this since they do not ethnically monitor applicants. This is a stale old excuse. Hundreds of black people are applying for jobs in journalism but are constantly rejected. Neither can media managers claim that black under-representation is due to lack of educational qualifications when ethnic monitoring in colleges shows that relatively more black people than white are entering further and higher education, and when most black people who apply for journalism jobs are graduates.

When journalism jobs are advertised in ethnic minority publications, there is a huge response by black people – as the BBC discovered. There is no lack of well qualified black people waiting for jobs in the media. Newspaper editors simply do not advertise in the ethnic press because jobs in nationals are highly competitive and vacancies are filled by word of mouth and because these papers clearly have no wish to employ black journalists.

I have spoken to dozens of black journalists, some with formal training, who have applied to national newspapers time and time again but have been turned down. Many did not even receive a reply to their applications. Some, however, do not apply to national papers because they see them as white and Oxbridge-orientated and generally closed to black people. Some believed that unless you have contacts in the nationals you do not stand a chance so it does not matter 'how good you are'.

Getting into national newspapers

Robin Lustig, former news editor of the *Observer,* observed in 1990 that 'nothing short of hustling by black and Asian journalists' will force national newspapers to change their employment patterns. His argument for why it is necessary for black people to hustle where whites do not is familiar:

> Too few black people apply for jobs and most papers don't advertise vacancies. They merely shift the applications already in their bulg-

ing file. Journalism is a highly competitive business. If you take out an ad, you are deluged with hundreds, perhaps thousands, of applications. Far easier to stick to the traditional method. It's not the way it should be but it's the way it is. (*Guardian* 12/11/90)

How does Lustig know that too few black people go for jobs when newspapers neither advertise jobs nor monitor applicants? And if newspapers do not advertise, how are black people going to know that there is a vacancy to apply for? Filling vacancies by word of mouth is a highly discriminatory practice and cannot be justified. Lustig advocated hustling as a way for black journalists to get onto national newspapers. He argued that a clever black journalist who is prepared to keep offering ideas, 'phoning in with tips, showing initiative and energy can get a job with the nationals'.

While hustling does sometimes help journalists get jobs, most staff journalists who are white are not reduced to this hustling. They are headhunted from local and provincial papers or taken from schools of journalism, and as very few black journalists have such opportunities they have less chance of getting staff jobs. Lustig went on to explain the ways in which journalists get into national newspapers:

There are three main ways journalists on national newspapers get their jobs: by being headhunted, by moving from casual freelance or shift working to a staff position, or by straight forward application. I got my first job on the *Observer* after working as a stringer for them and then writing to ask whether there was any chance of a more permanent position. By sheer fluke, there was and I stayed more than twelve years. (*Guardian* 12/11/90)

Lustig also suggested that black people should use contacts to get into national papers. But only a few black people have the contacts with powerful whites who are able to give them jobs or introduce them to the right people. For most black journalists the only way is by applying directly and this is the least successful. Lustig's three main ways of obtaining national newspaper jobs may work for whites but they are impractical for most black people. There is a *Catch-22* situation here. Black journalists cannot work as freelances or do shift work with newspapers if they have no training or newspaper experience, neither can they be stringers and, as we have seen, only a token few black people are taken into white journalism training. They are not head-hunted unless they have staff jobs and have proved themselves – and as most black journalists don't have staff jobs this is not possible either. National newspapers, like provincials, should be obligated to take on a certain number of the well qualified black journalists seeking employment. They should advertise jobs in the ethnic press, monitor staff and applicants by ethnicity, and have employment targets for non-white journalists.

Covering race stories

Getting a job on national papers is not the end of black journalists' problems. When they are employed some are expected to cover nothing but race stories. One journalist told me:

> I am qualified with provincial newspaper experience but when I went for a job they wanted me only to report on race stories covering muggings, rapes and immigration. I didn't take the job.

But not all journalists who are offered such restricted jobs by national papers refuse; many are thankful for any opportunity to work on a national paper.

> I did not care what the editor asked me to do – I would have said yes. All that mattered was that I was in, working for a national. How many black journalists get this opportunity? Anyway, I am proud to cover race stories. I am black so I have a better perspective than a white reporter. I know where the people involved are coming from so I have a better understanding of things.

Negative stories on race are a different matter and most black journalists feel uncomfortable writing them up. They fear the reaction of the black community if they are seen to be selling out. But one journalist who worked for a national Sunday paper told me that he had no qualms about 'shopping black people'. He was given a job because his first story was very well received. He investigated friends of his parents who were doctors and who he claimed were selling National Health Service drugs to India. He said:

> I don't care who it is, I just report what happens. My parents' friends were crooks so I exposed them. I had to move out of my community and my parents don't talk to me any more but writing the truth is more important.

Many stories written by this journalist over the years involved investigations into drug-trafficking in the Indian sub-continent. He was willing to be used to continue the newspaper's negative portrayal of black people. The paper was able to vindicate its story by pointing out that it was written by a black journalist. On the other hand, news is news wherever it come from and whoever writes it. There cannot be one rule for 'race stories' and another for the rest. Yet a common criticism of papers is that they give far less space to stories involving racism and crime against black people. And not all black journalists working for national papers are expected to do only race stories. As general reporters they cover the entire field, including those with a race dimension.

Some black journalists who work or have worked on national papers say that being black puts them under pressure. As one explained:

> I have been on this paper for several years but I feel always that I have to prove myself. They just don't think I am good enough. It's as if they are waiting for me to fail. They check everything I do. I don't know if they are doing this so that I can break and leave the paper, but I won't. Just the same, it is hard working here.

Another said: 'I am always looking over my shoulders because they are always watching and checking on what I do. They don't do this to whites.' But others disagree: 'Of course I am under pressure but so are white journalists. We have to find stories and work to tight deadlines'. 'I have to do my work to a high standard. My editor expects it and I expect it of myself. This is bound to create pressure and so colour has nothing to do with it.'

Black journalists not only want to work in the white media but they also want promotion. However, very few move from general reporter to political or overseas correspondent, even fewer are columnists and none so far has been promoted to editor of a provincial or national newspaper. There is not so much a glass ceiling but a cement ceiling. A black journalist on a national told me:

> I have worked as a general reporter for several years yet when a senior position comes up I am never even considered , yet young white men come in and I am supposed to show them the ropes, then they are promoted above me. My years of service count for nothing and because I am black I am supposed to be grateful.

Magazines

Literally hundreds of magazine titles are published in Britain each year and this should have created yet more opportunities for black people to train and work in journalism. But the story is the same: very few black people are employed by mainstream magazines. After writing to all the major magazines seeking information on the ethnic make-up of their staff I found only ten. Of the hundred magazine to which I wrote, seventy replied, saying either that they had no black journalists or, as one woman's magazine told me: 'We employ 200 editorial staff and of these one is Asian and another African'. The managing editor seemed proud of the fact that two of his editorial staff were black and did not seem to think that this was a remarkably small number. And indeed, this magazine was better than most, which did not employ a single black person on their editorial staff.

When asked why this was the case, the reply was familar – 'black people don't apply'. However, like newspapers, magazines do not undertake ethnic monitoring so have no idea whether or not black people apply. When I asked what the magazine is doing to get more black editorial staff, they replied, like the newspaper editors, that they take people on merit. They seem totally unaware that their employment practices might be discriminatory. One magazine editor was more candid:

> We rarely take people through straightforward applications, although pre-entry students who have done work placement on our magazine, if they are good and can fit in, we employ when they finish their course. Most of those we employ are already known to us either because we know their work or they are recommended.

Word of mouth employment is not only unfair – it is also difficult to prove. However, it is not impossible to stop such discriminatory acts, especially if the CRE was given power to investigate and take employers to tribunals for such discriminary procedures.

We have seen what can be done against racist employment practices when a group of black workers from Ford took the company to an industrial tribunal in 1997, claiming discrimination on grounds that only whites were given well-paid drivers' jobs. The company had allowed white drivers to bring in their kith and kin and so jobs were not fairly competed for. Ford had to pay their black workers £70,000 compensation. It is to be hoped that this will discourage employers, including those in the media, from employing people in this way.

Kathy Watson, an Oxford graduate, became the first black editor of a mainstream magazine *Woman's Realm* in 1995. She is important in demonstrating that with the right opportunities, black people can and do do well. Kathy Watson's advice to other black people who want to work on magazines is to 'apply for jobs' but in the meantime to...

> try and get some freelance work. If you are someone at school who thinks you would like to work in magazines... then get work placements in your holidays... it will give you an idea how magazines work which is going to help you get a job. (*New Impact*, April/May, 1996)

Her advice is that when a person gets a job in the media they should be prepared to start at the bottom and work their way up and 'show willingness'. Editors and heads of departments are looking for people who are 'willing to take on anything'. Kathy Watson explains that a new writer may have to write for nothing initially but that getting your work in print is important because as a prospective magazine journalist you are in a better position if you have something to show. Magazine jobs require writers who have varied interests and, of course, you have to learn to write.

However, both newspapers and magazines need to reflect the multi-racial, multicultural society that Britain is. The old excuses for black under-representation are untrue and no longer acceptable. Action needs to be taken and ethnic monitoring is the first step, followed by targeting. The CRE and black journalists' groups are well placed to give advice to newspapers and magazines on how to employ more black journalists. They should also sponsor black people into journalism training and employ once they are qualified.

Broadcasting

While less than fifty black journalists work in the mainstream print media, over 300 are employed in broadcasting. Although this includes those black journalists working on programmes made for a black audience, it is still relatively high compared with the print media. The difference is due to the broadcasting industry taking equal opportunities more seriously. Although some television and radio stations only pay lip-service to race equality, the broadcasting industry showed during the late 1980s and the early 1990s what can be achieved when equal opportunities procedures are implemented.

The BBC was the first to take measures regarding equal opportunities after its 1988 survey revealed that less than one per cent of its editorial staff were black. It made a commitment that eight per cent of its staff would be black by the year 2000. To redress the under-representation of black people in BBC-run journalism courses, the corporation set up three black-only journalism courses. Between 1988 and 1994 when the courses closed, the BBC trained and employed dozens of black journalists. Now that the black-only courses have gone the numbers of black journalists employed in the BBC and elsewhere in the industry will almost certainly diminish. London Weekend Television (LWT) also stated a commitment to targeting; in 1990 it publicly declared its hope that by the year 2000 ten per cent of its staff would be black – but they too have lost their momentum.

The increasing numbers of black newsreaders, presenters and reporters on our screens in the late 1990s are a result of broadcasting's direct action in equal opportunities. By the year 2000 the numbers will either remain the same or decrease because equal opportunities policies have been generally dropped. If black people and the media unions do not keep up the pressure for equal opportunities in practice, television will return to the bad old days when black people only appeared as maids, fools or involved in crime.

Employment in the black media

More than half of all black journalists in Britain work in the black media. It plays a vital role in providing employment and training for black people who have been turned down in the mainstream. Over 90 per cent of those black journalists especially in the press, have no formal journalism training or experience in the white media: they hope that whatever they gain from working in the black media will increase their chances of securing work in the mainstream.

Programmes made by television and radio for a black audience employ only black journalists except for the director or, in a very few instances, series-producers. It is not that these programmes do not want white journalists – more that white journalists are not attracted to these programmes because pay is relatively low. Black journalists applying to work on these programmes find that they compete only with other black applicants and some consider this an advantage 'because we don't stand a chance against white journalists. We just have the wrong colour.' Others think that although these programmes are for a black audience, white journalists should not be excluded: 'We should have to compete against whites for jobs. We should get the job because we are good, not because we are black.' Nevetheless these programmes give and have given aspiring black journalists the chance to work and learn broadcasting skills.

There have been several other criticisms of black-only programmes, mostly to do with the lack of training of those working on these programmes. These journalists ask for in-house training because they are aware of the mistakes they make and want black-only programmes to be professional and of a high standard. But the television companies concerned are reluctant to give in-house training and argue that journalists have to learn as they work. As one journalist commented: 'but we make a lot of mistakes because we have no training and it means that black-only programmes are unprofessional'.

Ebony, a programme made by the BBC in the 1980s, was one programme journalists mentioned as being below standard. It was also under-funded. One journalist, who tried to get training while working on the programme, explained:

> I worked on *Ebony* for a year and I had no journalistic training and I kept asking the BBC for short in-house training but neither me or anyone else on the programme got training.

Some journalists alleged that training was deliberately witheld because 'the BBC did not want to make the programme any better'. They wanted viewers 'to think that black people are incapable of making good programmes and so perpetuate the negative stereotype'. These views might appear cynical but there is reason for such suspicions when we know how pervasive racism is in society and how competitive television is.

In my opinion, many of the black-only programmes on television and radio, especially in the 1980s, were diabolical and even *Black On Black* and *Eastern Eye* were not always up to scratch. Although they gave work to many black journalists, these programmes were not only restricted in what issues they dealt with but used presenters who had very little experience – if any – in interviewing live on television. There have also been some well produced black-only programmes on television, especially in the 1990s, such as *Bandung File* and *Black Britons*, clearly indicates that black people, given the training and finance, are able to make highly professional television programmes.

Other problems can arise on black television and radio programmes if they have white series-producers. Journalists described these producers as 'not having a clue about what black people want to watch'. A black producer saw the problem this way:

> Although I produce the programme they try to tell me what black people want to watch and they are white and middle-class and don't know or care about black people's lives and experience. Often my decisions were undermined by the white series producer. Eventually I had to leave.

The pay on these programmes is described by journalists as 'a pittance' because radio and television stations put on black-only programmes on the cheap. Management do not treat these programmes or those who work on them seriously, because they are made for a black audience. One journalist told me that even the camera crew on one black-only programme treated the programme as a joke, calling it 'the wog prog'.

Despite the negative experience of many black journalists working on black-only programmes, some very talented individuals, such as Samir Shah and Trevor Phillips, have started in them and have made their way up the slippery ladder of television.

African-Caribbean publications

African-Caribbean publications in Britain go back to the early nineteenth century. Famous black authors of the time included Ignatius Sancho, Olaudah Equiano and Mary Seacole. In *The Black Press in Britain* (1995) Ione Benjamin explains the idea behind early African-Caribbean newspapers and journals:

In the early days black owned newspapers and journals were nearly all affiliated to an independent or political organisation, all campaigning for the liberation of Africa and the descendants of Africa. The news organ... articulated the woes and aspirations of millions of Africans and their descendants in Britain and around the globe. (1995, 11)

The foundations of the African-Caribbean press as it exists in Britain today were laid in the 1950s, with the *Jamaican Gleaner*, the *Caribbean News* and later the *West Indian Gazette*. While the *Gleaner* was considered right-wing, the *Caribbean News* was seen at the time as ultra-left (1995).

The *West Indian Gazette* was launched in 1958, the year of the Notting Hill disturbances. It was run and edited by the political activist Claudia Jones, who was world-renowned for her resistance to what she saw as political tyranny. During the Notting Hill riots against black people, Claudia Jones worked ceaselessly to get black people out of jail, and the *West Indian Gazette* was an important tool for information. It was:

designed to stimulate political and social thinking, to serve as a catalyst, quickening the awareness, socially and politically of West Indians, Afro-Asians and their friends. Its editorial stand was for a united and independent West Indies, full economic, social and political equality and respect for human dignity... for peace and friendship between all Commonwealth and world peoples. (1985, 82-83)

Other black individuals have since tried to follow Claudia Jones' example, setting up newspapers and magazines, but most have failed due to the high cost of publishing. The 1970s and '80s saw the launch of several African-Caribbean publications. For example, the *Caribbean Times,* begun in 1977, is still being published and was initially considered the leading African-Caribbean paper in Britain although now it is seen as representing the older immigrants. When the *Voice* newspaper appeared in 1982 the two papers became rivals, with the *Voice* presenting itself as the 'Best-selling black paper in Britain' and targeting young black Britons. In 1992 the management of the *Voice* newspaper published another newspaper called the *Journal*, designed to cater for black middle-class professionals, but by 1997 *New Nation* was competing in the same market.

Asian publications

Some publications aimed at the Asian community are in English and others are in the languages of the sub-continent. There are peculiarities and exceptions among various vernacular papers but in general they follow similar patterns in terms of production and distribution as well as in their approach to news. At the last count the CRE listed 32 vernacular publications in Britain catering for over 300,000 settlers of Asian origin. The major role of the vernacular papers is to unite immigrant communities. They have played an important role in maintaining psychological and community links among immigrants scattered across different parts of Britain and they help in maintaining the languages and cultures of the Indian sub-continent.

The political role of the vernacular press falls into two areas: first, the politics of the countries of their origin and, second, the politics of Britain. So the Punjabi press concentrates on news from the Punjab, the Gujarati press on news from Gujarat. As far as British politics are concerned, many of the Asian papers, like the African-Caribbean ones, concentrate on matters concerning the problems of race and immigration. Asian papers deal similarly with the cultural identity of Asians in Britain.

Working in black publications

African-Caribbean and Asian publications provide employment and training opportunities for aspiring black journalists. However, working in black publications is far from ideal; for instance, the pay and conditions are well below those of mainstream publications and to date there is no organised training in the black press. As one editor told me, 'We would like to organise training but we can't afford it.' Their sales are relatively small and they do not attract big company advertising. Such advertising as they get is either from small black businesses or from mainly left-wing councils.

Newspapers like the *Voice*, survive on advertisements from public bodies, especially local councils. During the 1980s these councils saw advertising in the ethnic press as part of their equal opportunities policy, and they still do. By advertising their jobs in black publications, public bodies are giving black people the opportunity to apply. But there is only a limited amount of advertising from public bodies and all the black publications are competing for it. The launch of *New Nation* only intensified the competition between black publications.

The financial difficulties which black publications experience result in many closing soon after they begin. One journalist, angry about her experience in the black press, said: 'The black press is doing a disservice to black journalists because they don't give proper training and we make a lot of mistakes'. Others question the view that the black papers are not making enough money to pay their journalists properly or provide proper training:

This is an excuse not to invest in training. I don't see the managers of these papers living in council houses. They all live in expensive houses in the suburbs. They should pay journalists the right wages. Maybe they can't pay national newspaper wages but they can do better than they do. They have a responsibility to sponsor black journalists into recognised courses and not just leave it to the NUJ or white papers.

Black journalists working in black publications believe that while the black media were important in helping black people to get some journalism training and experience, after a time, usually a year, they should move on. Consequently, the black media have a high staff turnover. Many journalists wanted to leave because 'My chances of promotion are slim', 'There are hardly any senior posts', 'It's a dead-end job and after a while you get frustrated', or 'the pay is crap'.

There is another disadvantage for journalists working in black publications: they usually experience discrimination when they apply for jobs in the mainstream. White editors generally discount any training or experience black journalists bring from their time in black publications. Some employers in the mainstream think working in black publications means that black journalists can only write 'black stories'. After they have received some training and experience in the black press, they are rejected again and black journalists can get caught up in this cycle of racism and eventually leave journalism. Even past editors of black publications have experienced difficulty getting jobs in mainstream media. One told me:

I have worked my way from being a reporter on a black newspaper to becoming its editor but when I applied for a job on mainstream I was told that they couldn't take me because I had no training. After ten years working on the paper I think I know all there is to know, so why should I need any more training? I believe all this is due to racism and the only way to counteract this is by a system of quotas for black people.

Black journalists who trained and worked abroad in Third World countries face similar discrimination to those working in the black media in Britain. The same reasons are given. White editors and managers regard the training and experience of black journalists achieved in a Third World country as inferior. Journalists explain: 'having had training and years of experience in India and the Far East as a journalist counted for nothing when I applied for a job in England.' Another said: 'I was a reporter for five years in Nigeria. I also did research and script writing but this was not good enough to get me a job in British papers or television.'

Despite the difficulties which black publications face and the criticisms sometimes directed at these publications, they are the life-line of the African-Caribbean and Asian communities. They do two important things: they give black people the opportunity to become publishers and journalists and, secondly and most importantly, black publications, especially the black press, campaign against racial injustice in Britain and the United States. These publications also promote positive black role models both alive and dead.

Although many black journalists who have worked for black publications have difficulty getting into the white media, others have shown that these difficulties can be overcome. What it takes is diligence and determination. A producer who had moved from the black press to television told me: 'I never gave up. I kept pestering them, sending in ideas. Eventually I was called in for interview and I never looked back.'

Black broadcasting in Britain

Ethnic minority broadcasting is as important as newspapers in terms of the training and employment of black journalists. It is seen and sees itself as having a general duty to work toward the elimination of racial discrimination and to promote equality of opportunity for black people. As Peter Newsam, ex-chair of the CRE explained:

> There are two main aspects of the relationship between the ethnic minorities and the media. The first concerns the way in which ethnic minorities are presented and portrayed. The second concerns the opportunities provided to the ethnic minorities, especially those who have difficulties with English, to obtain information, entertainment and cultural satisfaction from the media. (Newsam, 1983, 7)

But how does black broadcasting fulfil its role in training, employing people and promoting race-relations when broadcasting, especially television, is such an expensive medium? At present there are no national black-managed television stations in Britain. In 1993 two black-owned cable television stations started, one Asian and one African-Caribbean. By 1998 there were two Asian Cable Television stations but the African-Caribbean station closed due to lack of finance. In the United States by contrast, there are nine black-owned television stations, though this is a tiny proportion of the 1,000 television stations in the United States. Black radio stations are more numerous too. In the 1970s there were only 30 out of 9,000 but by the mid-1980s there were 200. Although black-owned newspapers have declined, 'the number of radio stations and magazines targeted to the black population has increased' (Wilson and Gutierrez, 1995).

One reason for the increase of black-owned radio stations in the United States is this:

> Proportionally blacks were found to be a more responsive audience than whites. As a result, astute advertisers were able to tap into a lucrative marketplace, often at the expense of traditional avenues including black newspapers and magazines. Many major co-operations were among those which sought to reach the ever expanding black buying power traced back to the black community. (Ploski and Williams, 1989, 276)

There are only a few fully licensed Black owned radio stations in Britain, although there are several fully or partly licensed radio stations which cater for African-Caribbean and Asian listeners. There are a number of Pirate stations which were a response in the 1980s to the need for black people to own and run radio stations. With readily available equipment, these stations provided programmes, mainly of music, for the young whose tastes were not catered for by mainstream white radio. By 1989, black pirate radio stations were given the opportunity to own and run their own stations legally, but most did not succeed in their bid for licensing. WNK Radio was the only successful one, but after four years broadcasting it lost its licence in 1994. Choice FM, which began in 1990, is one of the few radio stations in London providing a black perspective.

The history of black people in broadcasting is more recent than in the press. It dates back to Elizabeth Welch, a black actress and singer who had her own radio series with the BBC in 1934. Black people were also present at the opening of BBC television in 1936, where the American song and dance duo Buck and Bubbles starred in a variety show. During the late 50s and early 60s, the actor and calypso singer Cy Grant became one of Britain's first black television stars, appearing nightly on the BBC's *Tonight* programme singing the news in calypso. These were the stereotypical roles black people were offered in the new medium of television.

Actors Pearl and Edric Connor set up an agency to 'represent and promote black talent in Britain and to press for non-stereotypical roles for blacks in the performing arts' (Pines, 1992, 9). In the early years of television, there were some important landmarks such as John Elliot's *A Man From the Sun* in 1956, one of the first attempts to look at the 'West Indian immigrant experiences.. rather than focusing simply on the white British reaction to immigrants and immigration.' (Pines, 1992, 9)

Although such programmes were seen as radical, Jim Pines argues that they were only permitted by the television establishment to exist on the 'margins of mainstream programme making' and made 'precious little impact on overall institution thinking' (1992, 10). The early 1960s also saw a number of plays and television series which gave black actors the opportunity to work in mainstream drama even if only for a short time – *Coronation street* (1963), *Z Cars* (1964), *Passage To India* (1965) and

Fable (1967) which explored inter-racial relationships. The play *Rainbow City* dealt with a racially mixed marriage in Birmingham. Television then felt it was safe to portray different experiences of black people in Britain – but this was not to last.

In the late 1960s, after Enoch Powell's 'rivers of blood' speech, opportunities for black people in television drama and on the stage dried up. White broadcasting managers had become sensitive to the black presence in Britain and were linking blacks to 'problems' or, as Desmond Wilcox says, 'to a screaming level of prejudice' (1992, 12). Carmen Monroe talks about the difficulties she and many other black performers faced then:

> After three successful plays in the 1960s things started to dry up and suddenly I was doing nothing.. I felt as though I was being ignored, put away, shut up somewhere. (1992, 62)

Joan Hooley, who appeared in *Emergency Ward 10* in 1963, said that once she had been written out of the series she found that suddenly:

> For some unknown reason there wasn't any work around... all black actors and actresses were very concerned, we couldn't put our finger on the problem. None of our work was being put out. (1992, 100)

Pines maintains that this barren period was due to a 're-emerging sense of anxiety about the black presence' (1992, 12). During this racially sensitive period the only programme to feature racial themes was *Till Death Us Do Part* and this was achieved without many black actors. The anti-hero, Alf Garnett, was 'Enoch Powell's alter ego' but most importantly he represented white working-class racism at its worse.

The series was a hit – the majority of viewers could relate to Alf Garnett because he was expressing their deep-seated attitudes towards black people.

In the 1970s there were several multi-racial documentaries which set out to explain various aspects of so-called immigrant life. Black people and their life and culture were put under the microscope. These programmes were supposed to help combat racism, the idea being that if white British people understood why blacks had different cultures and languages it would make them more tolerant of the black presence. Programmes such as *In The Beautiful Caribbean* (1972), which showed black people in unstereotypical roles, were meant to be good for race relations. However, black television programmes of the 1970s were dominated by situation comedies such as *Love Thy Neighbour, The Fosters* and *Mixed Blessings*.

The comedy *Love Thy Neighbour,* which ran from 1972-1975, was brought on as a demonstration of 'balance' to *Till Death Us Do Part.* Black actor Rudolph Walker, who became nationally famous for his role as Bill Reynolds, the self-assured black neighbour of the 'irritating white bigot' Eddie Booth (Jack Smethurst) in *Love Thy Neighbour*, said that at his audition and interview for the part he laid down certain conditions: 'I would only do the part if my character wasn't made into an 'Uncle Tom''. He insisted that if his white neighbour hit him, 'I would hit him back' (1992).

The 1980s saw the emergence of a number of black-led television programmes which gave training and employment to black people. They included *Skin* (1980), *Eastern Eye* and *Black On Black. Skin* was a series of half-hour documentaries described as for and about the African-Caribbean and Asian Communities in London. The series helped the career progression of two well-known black people in television, Trevor Phillips, past editor and presenter of the *London Programme* and Samir Shah, now part of the senior management of BBC news and current affairs directorate.

The problem with programmes such as *Skin* was that they focused on the black stereotypes without looking at black people as an integral part of society. The time allocated for these prorammes was not enough for them to deal with the issues of black people in any meaningful way. Asian and African-Caribbean experiences also needed to be dealt with separately – as they are today.

Channel 4 was the first mainstream television channel to institute equal opportunity policies in its programming when it started in 1982. The channel ran two important current affairs programmes for black people: *Eastern Eye* and *Black On Black.* Although the decision to produce these programmes came under criticism from some quarters, the programmes were generally liked by black viewers. They dealt with current affairs and the experiences of the communities in Britain. Eventually the programmes proved inadequate: they failed to explore racism in Britain and the black experience in any meaningful way, concentrating instead on safe subjects such as music, fashion and food.

When in 1985 Farrukh Dhondy became the new commissioning editor for Channel 4 ethnic minority programming, *Black on Black* and *Eastern Eye* were scrapped. Instead, Dhondy commissioned Tariq Ali's new independent production company, *Bandung File*, to produce African-Caribbean, Asian and or Third World news and current affairs. But *Bandung File* generally looked at news and current affairs in non-white countries and rarely at racism in Britain and America, so it was no different from earlier black-led programmes. It too was later scrapped too and nothing has been put in its place, although there have been regular documentaries about Third World countries on Channel 4, many presenting negative portrayals of black people and their countries.

For example, in 1997 a four-part series on Channel 4 covered Kingston Public Hospital in Jamaica. It presented the city of Kingston as a war zone with hundreds of killings from guns and knives. The hospital at the centre of the programmes was presented as unable to cope, due to lack of facilities such as operating theatres and shortages of drugs and blood for transfusion. The programme was so negative that the Jamaican ambassador complained.

The mainstay of Channel 4's black-related drama is situation comedy. Although these programmes have been written and produced by black people, the Channel has been criticised for limiting black imagery to comedy. As Norman Beaton, who was one of the best known black British actors, observed:

> There are very serious black people out there but these roles are not being written. This is either because the white man does not understand where black people are coming from and therefore doesn't know how to write about black people; or it's because we black people don't have the confidence in our own existence and destiny, so we are not writing that kind of material for ourselves.(1992, p10)

The American media

Although there is a lack of research and general interest in the under-representation of black people in the British media, this is not true of the United States. A survey of American Society of Newspaper Editors (ANSE) found that African-Americans represented 21 per cent of the United States population but only seven per cent of broadcast and print news staff, and that nearly 60 per cent of America's newsrooms employ no African-Americans (ANSE, 1989). While the percentage of black people hired in other industries improved in the 1980s, the numbers in the news media have increased only slightly since the late 1960s. In 1968, the *Report of the National Advisory Commission on Civil Disorders* (The Kerner Commission) reported that less than five per cent of America's journalists were black or Hispanic and that most newspapers provided poor overall coverage of black community issues.

In response to the Kerner Commission's findings, the ANSE set a goal to attain minority representation in newsrooms in proportion to the US minority population by the year 2000. It is hard to imagine newspaper or broadcast management even suggesting this in Britain when they deny that there is a race problem in the media. However, it was not until 1985 that the organisation formed the ANSE Task Force, designed to encourage minorities in newspaper journalism training and jobs.

During the 1970s the numbers of black and Hispanic journalists rose in the American media because of pressure from the federal government and the black community. Leaders of Cincinnati's African-American community, for example, pressured local television stations in 1972 to hire more on-camera black people, threatening to call in the Federal Communications Commission (FCC), which requires every television station to provide a service to the community if it wants to keep its operations license. However, Reagan and then Bush, stopped pushing affirmative action and fewer black journalists have been able to get jobs in America's white media.

In 1988, the first survey of racial minorities and women was carried out by the American Newspaper Publishers Association (ANPA). It showed that very few black people were employed as journalists, although they made up 16 per cent of newspaper employees – most were in clerical and service positions. As in Britain, women fared better than black people with 37 per cent working as newspaper journalists. The report found that even fewer were employed in management positions: only five per cent were African-Americans. The decision-making in the newsroom was dominated by whites, with 95 per cent as newsroom supervisors, 93 per cent in copy desk positions and 91 per cent as reporters and writers.

Another report on America's media undertaken by Professor Vernon Stone, *Pipelines and Dead-End Jobs Held by Minorities and Women in Broadcast News* (1988), found that by the late 1980s there was a drop in the numbers of ethnic minority men in the United States media, from ten per cent in 1979 to eight per cent in 1986. The reason was:

...their lack of professional advancement. They are under-represented in supervisory positions and are not even in the pipeline for management. Instead they are most often photographers and can easily remain so on a dead-end basis. (Stone, 1988, 5)

Seventy-one per cent of black and Hispanic journalists in America are frustrated by the way their paper covers issues concerning race. They argue that race issues are either marginalised or poorly reported.

Nor are racial discrimination and retention of black journalists in America's media confined to newspapers. Randy Daniels, a black journalist, left his job at *CBS News* after nearly ten years because he saw no career advancement opportunities in the network:

I met with every level of management at *CBS News* over issues that specifically relate to Blacks and other minorities... when it became clear to me that such meetings accomplished nothing, I chose to leave and work where my ideas were wanted and needed. I have found my race an impediment to being assigned major stories across the entire spectrum of news. (1995, 209)

By contrast the employment of white women increased in television – from 26 per cent in 1972 to 32 per cent in 1979. More women in America also moved up into managerial positions in television and radio. 'Female television directors increased from one per cent in 1972 to 14 per cent in 1986' (Stone, 1988). It is evidently easier for media employers and others to deal with gender than race equality and many, when having to deal with equality issues, go for the safer option of giving equality to women. This is not to say that women are not in a disadvantaged position and also need equal access to training and jobs but I believe the real challenge for employers is to deal with black equality.

Until the mid-1980s white America's newspaper editors were openly hostile to the idea of hiring non-white journalists. The American Society of Newspaper Editors Survey (1982) found that editors held racist views about black people and thought that hiring non-white journalists would 'lower the standard' of their newspapers. One editor told the survey that:

> generally hiring minorities means reducing standards temporarily, except for one reporter and one news editor, every minority person we've hired in 10 years was less qualified than a concurrently available white. (1994, 209)

America's ethnic minorities were given the opportunity to train as journalists during the 1980s as part of the country's affirmative action policy. Can the efforts of the 1980s to create a multicultural media be sustained in the 1990s as US economic fortunes sag? There have been staff lay-offs and closures of newspapers and network television news bureaux. And can American media keep black journalists once they are hired? In Britain, there are similar worries, as staff jobs in the media are reduced because of the need for more profit. This has affected the employment of black journalists in mainstream media. As they are the last to be employed, they are the first to go.

CHAPTER 5

BLACK WOMEN IN THE MEDIA

Black Women are the true Pioneers of the Women's Movement. They have always known what it takes to move mountains. Uncommon courage. Unparalleled creativity. Unwavering commitments. They don't know the meaning of can't and have never accepted the concept of 'impossible'. (*Ebony*, August, 1991)

Although the women's movement has been led by white women in America and Britain this does not mean that black women were not interested in feminist resistance to male chauvinism. Rather, it shows that racism has made it almost impossible for black women to lead. Historically Black women have experienced more sexual oppression than any other female group but were powerless to organise any collective resistance to racism and sexism. As black women we have had to work to look after ourselves and our children because slavery, colonisation and racism made it almost impossible for us to depend upon black men to support us. Emigrating to 'the motherland' has not altered our position all that much: we are still faced with sexism and racism.

Despite the vast contribution that black women have made in Britain and worldwide we have largely been ignored, especially in education and employment. We are perceived as either 'victims or superwomen' but we are neither. We are women who, because of double discrimination have learnt how to survive. As Hazel Carby declares:

> The black woman critique of history has not only involved us in coming to terms with absences, we have also been outraged by the ways in which it has made us invisible, when it has chosen to see us. History has constructed our sexuality and our femininity as deviating from those qualities with which white women, as the prize objects of the Western world, have been endowed. We have also been defined in less than human terms. (1982, 212)

Women in employment

Before the 1975 Sex Discrimination Act very few women chose to work as journalists and even fewer were admitted into this white middle-class male domain. The 1977 Press Commission did not even trouble to consider the complaints put to it that women were being discriminated against in newspapers. Women were not regarded as an important part of the media. By the 1990s the situation had changed. Nearly 50 per cent of those applying for membership to the NUJ were women and the Newspaper Society also found that the numbers of women enquiring about journalism courses had increased. In some sectors of the media, for example freelance and magazines, there are more women than men. I found that there were more black women journalists employed in the media than men: 56 to 44 per cent, but this is changing as more full-time jobs in the media are lost.

How do black women fit into the generally racist and sexist atmosphere of the media? Some black male journalists believe that black women are given preferential treatment. One thought that 'black women are having it easier to get media jobs than men, especially in television, because they are more attractive to white males'. While this might be true in some cases, these male critics say nothing about the education and skills of black women journalists working in television. In the end it does not matter how physically attractive a woman on television is – if she cannot do the job she is out.

Judging women by their physical attraction and not by skills and intelligence is typically male. For the fact is that black women journalists are more likely to get on screen or into mainstream journalism because they are better educated and more have journalism training than black men do (Ainley, 1994).

However, it is not possible to look at women's position in the media without first looking at the changes in the labour market, particularly the situation of black women since their arrival after the Second World War. Women's position in employment has varied since the industrial revolution. But what has not changed is that women's work is still not taken seriously. When a woman is married and working, her wage is called a 'second income' even though these wages are an integral part of most families' income and even though, without them, there would be more children living at or below the poverty line in Britain, which presently stands at 30 per cent.

In the early phases of Britain's industrial revolution 43 per cent of women were employed (1885 census). Jobs were mainly in domestic service, textiles, mills and factories. By the beginning of the 20th century the numbers of women in paid employment began to decline. This was due to discrimination: women were treated as incapable of doing men's jobs, a strategy which kept women dependent upon men. The Victorians asserted that a woman's place was in the home. Women who worked were treated as social outcasts because it was argued, as it is still in some quarters today, that women who worked were not 'good mothers'.

Women's employment changed during the First World War. They were expected to do so-called men's work when their husbands went to the trenches. Women worked in engineering and the explosives industry, earning high wages and freedom from the kitchen sink. But after the war they were sent back home and again told they could not do 'men's work'. The pattern was repeated after the Second World War but this time women refused to return passively to domesticity. They were aware of their potential and knew they were good as or better than men.

After the Second World War expansion of world economies and the service sector meant that there were more opportunities for women to enter the job market. Between 1951 and 1971, 2.5 million extra workers were taken on in Britain and 2.2 million were women. By 1977, 40 per cent of the labour force was female and in the 1990s two thirds of women go out to work. But the jobs most women do are in the service industries and are low-paid, low status and part-time (EOC, 1994).

The 1960s brought not only a sexual revolution but the desire of women to break the barriers preventing them from gaining careers and well-paid jobs. Because women had to fit their careers around men, child-rearing and 'duties' towards the older generation, opportunities for self-development were previously not even thought of. Simone de Beauvoir argued that a woman's life doesn't really begin until after the menopause, while Gloria Steinem, writing 30 years later, took a similar view: 'It is perhaps only in old age, certainly past fifty, that women can stop being female impersonators and can grasp the opportunity to reverse their most cherished principles of femininity.' (*Every Woman*, 1995)

Black women in Britain

Black women's experience of work, paid or otherwise, began no in post-war Britain but with slavery and colonisation. This is one fundamental difference between white women and black – a difference not accepted by many in the women's movement because they wanted to believe that all women had the same struggle. They did not recognise that racism played a greater part in the lives of black women than sexism. During slavery, black women were soon found to be capable of back-breaking work in the fields and work as domestics, nannies and seamstresses. In the eyes of the slave master black women 'were equal to men just as long as our strength matched theirs' but were more than equal to their men because 'having completed our work on the estate it fell to us to tend to the children and perform domestic duties' (Bryan *et al*, 1985).

Black women in their countries of origin were more recently used to doing both paid and unpaid work. Some also held professional jobs, such as teachers and nurses, while others ran their own businesses. Though some of the jobs black women did in their countries of origin were hard and low-paid, they gave the women financial independence.

Many Asian women were in work before they arrived in Britain. It has been estimated that over a third of Indian women are active in the labour market and this does not include the women working at home or in the industrial sectors or the military (EOC, 1994). It is said that over 80 per cent of economically active women in India are involved in agriculture but many are also employed in catering and the food industry (Morgan, 1984). In rural areas of Pakistan many women work by taking care of animals, processing food, weaving and sewing and so contribute to their families' income.

Black women also served King and Country during the Second World War, although this fact is hardly ever acknowledged on Remembrance Day. Like white British women they were recruited in factories making bombs and aircraft and helping the war effort. This was not the only time that black women gave services to Britain – Mary Seacole, a Jamaican nurse, ran a hospital for British soldiers in the Crimean War. But it was Florence Nightingale, a white nurse, who received recognition and fame, while Mary Seacole was forgotten by British historians. It was only when two librarians reissued the book she wrote about her life (Seacole, 1978) that this great woman's work and dedication was recognised.

Coming to Britain hardly changed the lives of many black women. They were used to double work all their lives, both inside and outside the home. But here, in addition, there was racism. Many who came in the 1960s had had little or nothing to do with whites so had never before encountered direct racial discrimination in their country of origin.

Women who came from poor families had no means of getting education or skills and were expected to do domestic work. My own mother grew up in the rural part of Jamaica and her parents died when she was young. She was brought up by an older brother but had to leave when she was a teenager, joining the growing numbers of people fleeing to the towns in search of jobs. She ended up doing domestic work because she had neither the education nor the means to train for a decent job. Like many others of her generation, when Britain called for workers to rebuild the war-torn country, she seized the chance to go to 'the promised land'.

Domestic work in Jamaica did not pay very well and my mother had to save and borrow money to come to Britain. After some years she was able to send for me and my brother to join her in Britain. My father had long given up any responsibility for us since he had left when I was only one year old. In Britain, my mother, and other black immigrant women, had to take what jobs they were given – in the service industry, catering, cleaning tables, or working in sweat-shops unprotected by unions. Not only were black women not able to get decent well-paid jobs but they had difficulties finding accommodation, especially if they had children. It was not long before women like my mother began to realise that Britain was not the land of opportunity that black immigrants had been led to believe before they came here.

Black women experienced not only racism but sexism. Like black men, they had hoped to spend a few years in Britain, then return home with enough money to live. But for most this was a dream which never materialised. The wages they earned did not allow them to save and return. Even those who were skilled did not get the employment they wanted – they were given jobs that white women did not want. The work that black immigrant women did was an extension of the work they had done under colonisation. One woman explained her plight:

I have had lots of jobs since coming to this country. My first job when I arrived in 1960 was working as a chamber maid. I was bored with the work and the pay was bad, five pounds per week and I had to pay three shillings a week for fares and they kept a third of my wages for tax and insurance. I asked for a raise and they sacked me. (1988, 93)

Despite the thousands of black women working in the NHS since the 1960s for example, their work has not been rewarded by promotion or recognition by government or NHS managers. Without their contribution over the years the NHS would have collapsed. Maxwell observed that:

Consciously and unconsciously white supremacy in the more desirable jobs perpetuates itself. Blacks are apparently all very well in the kitchen staff and as SENs but not as managers and SRNs. Blacks are subjected to recruitment and selection procedures which they suspect to be unfair. (*New Community*, 1988, 445)

Black women and education
As we have seen, the education and skills of black immigrant women coming to Britain in the 1950s and 60s varied. While many were unskilled or semi-skilled, others had worked as teachers, nurses and administrators in their own country but were given low-paid jobs in Britain. Black women in the 1960s and beyond were also accused of causing their children to fail at school, while the state ignored racism in education and society. The educational under-achievement of black children, especially those of African-Caribbean descent still creates a great deal of controversy. But what is missing from the debate is the educational achievement of black girls as compared with boys. As Mirza notes:

Despite the educational success of African-Caribbean girls as compared to boys, they have been virtually ignored in race and gender research. (1992, 11)

Because of their gender and race black girls have been marginalised in educational research and stereotypical models were applied such as the 'passive' Asian mother unable to speak English and always at home and the dominating African or Caribbean mother always out of the home working (Carby, 1982). Culture and conflict were applied to girls more than boys. A government report in 1969 referred to what they saw as the rigid discipline of Asian households in which Asian girls were trapped. The report from the Select Committee on Race Relations and Immigration (1969) suggested that Asian women were the victims of this process and their own 'passivity'. In addition, Asian children were seen to have language problems, to suffer from over-ambition and to be victims of inter-generational conflict. Children of African-Caribbean descent were viewed as having 'chips on their shoulders', under-achieving, being aggressive and lacking in parental guidance (Mcdonald, 1990).

Brah and Dean (1986) found that young women, black and white, had a subordinate role in schooling. Girls are encouraged and expected to choose the arts and social sciences, while boys are encouraged to do maths and science. They also pointed to the invisibility of women in the curriculum and the failure of many teachers to take women's contributions seriously.

The relatively few studies done on black girls, experiences in education (Macdonald, 1990, Kelly and Cohen, 1991 and Mirza, 1992) show that they suffer sexism and racism through name-calling, violence and low teacher expectations. While black boys aggressively challenge the racist educational system, most black girls use well thought-out strategies which avoid 'the effects of racist and negative teacher expectations', refusing to take certain subjects or not asking for help. But some do openly challenge the system like boys and leave school without qualifications.

Mac an Ghaill (1988) describes a group of Asian and African-Caribbean girls who called themselves the 'Black Sisters'. They were 'pro-education' but not 'pro-school'. At school they showed limited resistance, which was carefully measured so as to avoid open conflict with teachers. Their resistance was against racism not education. Wilson (1978) describes the cultural conflict Asian girls are subjected to, particularly at school. Many have little to discuss with white girls, whose conversations revolve around boyfriends.

Whether black girls leave school without qualifications or not, many are returning to further and higher education. The Department for Education and Employment (DfEE) found that 20 per cent of black females have been through higher education as compared with 15 per cent of black men. And more black women than white enter further and higher education. It may be that they are aware of the double discrimination and difficulties they face in career choices. Or it may be that black girls from African-Caribbean backgrounds have been influenced by their mothers' orientation to work and education. As Mirza (1992) sees it:

> West Indian migrant women were influenced by their parents' orientation to work and education and that positive attitude towards education and the lack of constraint on female labour-market participation within West Indian families was found to account in part for young black women's high social class aspiration. (1992, 191)

As Pratibha Parmar has pointed out, careers officers do not offer Asian girls the same interviews and job opportunities as white girls. This is because they believe that Asian girls will be forced into marriage immediately after leaving school.

The common-sense logic of this racism dictates that a career for Asian girls is thought to be a waste of time (Parmar and Mirza October, 1981). However, black women journalists told me that they ignored such advice and instead found the information they wanted in books or from media unions.

Having reached university, black women face other ordeals. They often find themselves in isolation, especially if they are studying at an older university which takes only a few black students and can feel alienated in a higher education system which, like secondary education, has institutional racism. Yvonne Channer (1995) found that the negative experiences black children had in schools are often repeated and aggravated in higher education because the lecturers are predominantly white, male and middle-class. Black women have the worst time of all. A black women related her experience at one of the older universities:

> I was a phenomenon, the first and only black African-Caribbean woman in the department. Yes, there was racism on the part of the lecturers in a subtle way. I found the experience with the students in my year harrowing for a number of reasons: race was part of it, also the class factor. They were constantly gob-smacked by me. It was very much an experience of not listening to what I was saying but looking at me, my physical appearance. (1995, 90-91)

Although I did my first degree in a polytechnic I had similar experiences. I did an English language and literature degree, which was not popular at the time with black students, who were mostly doing sociology or B.Ed. and there were only three black students in my department. I was a mature student and I made friends with other mature students, who were generally friendly. My problem was with male lecturers who could not relate to me nor I to them. They did not understand where I was coming from – my poor working-class background, the double discrimination I faced and the fact that I had returned to education after fifteen years. But they feared me, not just because I did not fit the stereotype but because I was a strong black woman who questioned their views and ideas – with the result that I received very little help with my studies.

By my second year I was completely alienated from my white tutors and I never asked for help for fear of rejection. Instead I sought answers from books and other students. I had problems writing essays because I had been out of education for so long. My personal tutor told me that I needed to improve my essay-writing but never told me how. As I was determined to get my degree, I looked around for help and found that the college had study skills courses, which I did to improve my work. The discrimination most black women experience in further and higher education does not stop most of them from achieving in these institutions. Seeing our mothers and grandmothers going through the same life experience and surviving gives us the courage to buck the system and stand on our own two feet.

The portrayal of women by the media

The media's portrayal of women as bodies rather than minds and as caretakers rather than decision-makers, has become a normal part of society and helps to maintain their subordination. Despite the Sex Discrimination Act of 1975, women still earn less than men and very few are found in the boardrooms of Britain's leading industries. Even with a surge of new MPs less than a third are women.

'Determined by their own fantasies, the men who control the media attempt to control womankind' (*Out of focus*, 1987). Women are portrayed not as complex human beings but as sex objects to be used for pleasure and profit, as whores – or as mothers. We are used to sell commodities and encouraged to buy them. The media are powerful intruders in women's lives in a society which depends upon women's oppression to survive.

An article published in the *Evening Standard* carried the headline 'Career Women Make Men a Flop in Bed' (16/4/96). The story was based on a study carried out by *Relate* which found that men were complaining about impotence more than any other disorder. The reason, the paper claimed, was that men were stripped of their masculinity by career women. The blame was put firmly on women and the notion of gender equality. What is threatening for our patriarchal society is that the independent woman will not put up with useless men and in the 1990s a number of women are choosing to stay single, rather than live with men who treat them as second-class citizens.

It is not only women who are attacked for wanting equality but also men who support this notion. The headline of another article in the *Evening Standard* summed up their view of the equal man: 'Help! I am Married to a New Age Man'. The article was critical of men who share domestic responsibilities with their partners. An expert was quoted to confirm the view that men who helped their partners did more harm than good. Sandra Wheatley of the academic Department of Psychiatry at Leicester General Hospital said that women most likely to suffer from post-natal depression have partners who have been emotionally supportive, particularly during their pregnancy. The message was clear: women are better off without men's emotional support. Can it be that certain writers find it easier to accept male violence against women than the idea of a caring man?

The food and slimming industries have benefited from the stereotyped image of women perpetuated by the media. Women are judged by their age, appearance and what they wear. The perfect woman is slim, odourless, beautiful, youthful and white – the idea of a beautiful African woman seems to be a contradiction in terms. Billions of pounds are made each year in Western countries from diets, diet foods and drugs directed at women. The Women's Monitoring Network declared:

> All our affluent society's guilt about food is focused on women. Our society admires but cannot achieve abstemiousness. Thin women are fashionable partly because they seem to represent this elusive quality of self discipline, (and also because the apparent powerless-

ness of their emaciated bodies suits a patriarchal society like ours, in which men are the ones with strength and power). Women have little control over these values but they cause us great anxiety about food. (1987, 176)

Older women are almost invisible in the media and when they are seen they are portrayed negatively as the 'ailing dependent, the economic liability, the medical problem, the safety hazard' (1987). Many women internalise society's judgement of them whereas what older women need are positive images which reflect their varied lives and show that older women do not dwindle but flourish with age.

Women working in the media
Despite the increasing numbers of women coming into the media, they are still not treated equally with men. The differences in salaries speak for themselves: the average salary in newspapers is £32,000 for men compared with £22,500 for women (NUJ, 1996). The worst sector is the national newspapers, where only 19 per cent are women. Discrimination against women journalists is also evidenced in the jobs they are given. The great majority of women writers do feature articles on soft subjects such as children, relationships, food and fashion. Very few report on hard news or sport.

There are even fewer women working as overseas correspondents – Kate Adie is in a tiny minority. Both newspapers and television stations have begun using women to report sports and finance but still only rarely. The media industry is generally sexist, practising what it preaches.

In the 1990s two women became the editors of national papers, one a weekly tabloid, the other a Sunday tabloid. Georgina Henry came nearest to becoming editor of a national broadsheet in 1995, when she became deputy editor of the *Guardian*. Not only newspapers are guilty of sexism – most women working in television are found working as researchers or as assistant producers, glorified secretaries for mainly male producers. – who get the glory and the pay. A survey by *Skills Search* (1990) concluded that:

in television, video and films, the industry was predominately male. Three-quarters of broadcast employees, two-third of freelances and television journalists were men. (1990, 20)

Television is better paid and seen as more glamorous so very few women are given the opportunity to compete with men for the plum jobs. The women who do work in television are under such pressure from the combination of long and erratic hours and short-term contracts that they delay having children until they are well into their thirties or forties, or remain childless. The British Film Institute (1994) surveyed 319 people working in television and found that two-thirds of men in the study had children, against only 30 per cent of the women. Of the over-40s 53 per cent of women had no children, compared to 15 per cent of the men. Women journalists were afraid to have children because:

> There isn't room in the television industry at the moment to want both children and a career. There is no maternity leave. When you are working freelance you are working month to month. Suppose I am working 8-10 at nights, how does that fit in with a family? (British Film Institute, 1994)

A production assistant corroborated this: 'If I had a family I would have to change my job. I am always away filming.' Another said, 'many of the directors who are men are able to visit their families in between filming but we have to stay in the hotel and type up notes'. Men do not have to choose between their career and their families because they are not expected to look after children. This is made worse in television by the long unsocial hours people have to work and the fact that most media organisations do not provide nurseries.

Some women choose to remain childless because they feel that they could not combine work with family commitments. Television pro-gramme-maker Janet Street-Porter said she never wanted children be-cause working patterns on national newspapers and television are 'not conducive to having children' (the *Independent*, 5/12/1994). The BFI report found that some women who work in the media are fearful least their having children will count against them in jobs and promotion. Media women working on short-term contracts or as freelancers get no maternity leave. The media should be setting an example to the rest of society by providing nurseries and paid maternity and paternity leave to all employees. The new technology should enable employees to work from home or have flexible hours which suit family life.

Media managers appear unable to recognise the advantages of parenthood. Staff who have children are very much in touch with the basic reality of life and what is important to all of us. Having children helps men too if they share the care and responsibilities of their home and families. It is especially important for those who are making programmes about children and young people to be parents themselves and draw on their own experience.

Black women working in the media

Black women who choose to work in the media have to compete with white men, white women and black men – a formidable task. In the 1990s, black women are choosing middle-class occupations such as journalism, law and teaching, careers which are still seen by society as a white, middle-class domain. Many are refusing to bow to the stereotyped image society and the media impose upon them. For instance, very few are choosing nursing as an occupation. Despite low expectations from society, there are more black women graduates than men and more black women in the media than black men. My study found that more black women were accepted into mainstream journalism training than black men. However, this does not mean that black women have an easier time getting training.

Many of the black women journalists I spoke to who were accepted into mainstream journalism courses were exceptional. A television producer told me, 'Being a black woman who went to Oxford gave me a distinct advantage'. Another said, 'I went to a private school, then to Cambridge where I received a first-class degree in European languages. So it was not hard to get into a course.' But she was the exception. A newspaper reporter told me:

> It's not easy to get onto journalism training if you are a black woman because you have to compete with everyone. I tried for three years before I was successful and many times I felt like giving up especially after so many rejections. But I didn't because I wanted to become a journalist.

Others were accepted into journalism courses because they were in the right place at the right time. In the mid- to late-1980s some schools of journalism were under pressure to take on black students where they had none and a token number of black women were taken on. Those who had the opportunity rightly took full advantage of the situation. A black woman radio producer explained:

> I was accepted into journalism training without much problem because I deliberately applied to a particular course because I knew they had publicised themselves as equal opportunities employers and I also knew that they did take on a lot of women.

Another journalist told me,

> I was already working for this radio station and I knew that they sponsored staff for training. I also knew that they had no black people on their courses and that the CRE had criticised them so they were looking to redress the balance, so I applied and was welcomed.

Over 90 per cent of black women journalists have a degree, as compared to 60 per cent of black men, but this does not always act in their favour. The media do not appear to like intelligent black women because it goes against the stereotype. The men who control the media are afraid of intelligent women, especially if they are black, because they see us as a threat to a society which regards black women as inferiors. A black woman journalist stated:

> I have three degrees and I can't get into mainstream journalism training. They tell me I am too qualified, but what they mean is that they don't want an intelligent black woman because we are not supposed to be like this, we are supposed to be thick.

There are other ways for black women and men to get journalism training when conventional training schools close their doors. They can work voluntarily in a newspaper, magazine, radio, or television station in return for training. There are also short-term journalism courses in colleges and universities and correspondence courses are another alternative for those determined to learn journalism skills. Many of the black women journalists I spoke to tried a combination of these approaches. One told me, 'I did a two year correspondence course and, although I would have preferred to get on to a proper course, it helped me a lot.' Another said, 'All I could do was a twelve week evening course on freelance journalism because I had a child and could not get child care. But I had to do several short courses as well before I could write and sell my articles.'

Images of black women

The 1990s have seen a rise in the numbers of black women presenters on television, but while this trend is going in the right direction, in other areas of the media black women are still invisible. The only black women, apart from news readers and presenters, that we see frequently on television are superstars such as Naomi Campbell and Tina Turner but we also need to see the media portraying ordinary black women who have achieved.

At the time when relatively more black women are graduates and more are taking up white collar occupations we are still portrayed, if at all, in limited stereotyped roles such as dancers, singers and sports stars. We seldom see black women portrayed in television as lawyers, doctors, journalists, or politicians, jobs which they do in life.

Many black women are influenced by such presence in the media of women like Moira Stewart, who has been on BBC television for over fifteen years. It is beneficial not only for black people but for showing the white majority that black women have the qualifications and are capable of doing professional jobs. But do these women provide a cultural image for black women to identify with? These black women presenters do not differ in their dress or speech from white women presenters. Media managers are eurocentric and certainly do not want to put forward any other cultural image but the European. If a black woman is to succeed in any other occupation outside sports and music she...

> must dress, think, talk and act white. In other words she must first lose all sense of her black cultural identity if she wishes to find acceptance from the mainly white audience which determine TV ratings in this country. (1985, 194)

This is not to say that black women presenters have lost all sense of cultural identity. Those I spoke to are well aware of who they are and proud of their cultural backgrounds. Working on television is simply a job.

Black women, whether they are presenters or not, are expected to live up to the perfect image of womanhood which is presented as white. The glossy magazines especially perpetuate the sexist, racist order of things. They:

typify a specific caricature of modern woman for women en masse to emulate and assimilate. The new ideal woman is white, confident and partnered. She has a dulux gloss but hard as nails coating to hide any possible irregularities or realities as she strides purposefully forwards, her mission consumate. (*Guardian* 2/9/85)

This idealised version of womanhood has a more insidious effect upon black women than on white. In her efforts to emulate the image of white womanhood she spends, as Onwurah says,

twice as much in order to achieve a double impossibility to be perfect and to be white and this is probably why on average, black women spend more than white women on cosmetics in spite of the predictable differences in income. (*Guardian*, 2/9/85)

Some black women have internalised the concept that white is best, turning to lightening skin creams to make them more acceptable even though they can be dangerous and leave scars. At the other extreme are the women who refuse to use creams and those of African and Caribbean descent who choose to wear locks. Most black women are well aware of who they are but, like white women, are subjected to media images of beauty.

What the television companies have done is to put most of its black women journalist employees on screen, to give the impression that it employs a significant number of black people, but in reality fewer than two per cent per cent of black journalists work in television newsrooms. In newspapers and magazines there are even fewer. Most black women working in the media are concentrated in the lowest paid jobs with least decision-making. Even the glamorous black women presenters have little power because someone else generally writes their scripts. Those few positions of authority allocated to black people in television usually go to black men. Twice as many black men are employed by national dailies and Sundays than black women (Ainley, 1994).

Sexism in the media also affects black women in relation to the jobs they are offered. A black woman who wanted to be a sports reporter related:

I have always wanted to be a sports reporter since I was ten but I was laughed at by everyone I told. Many rightly pointed out that they had never seen a black sports reporter never mind a black woman. But I was determined to change this. After journalism training I applied for jobs as a sports reporter but never got anywhere and I know that this was because I am a black woman. I was told at one interview that 'coloured women don't apply for such jobs'. Eventually I managed to get some freelance work covering a football match and I had a horrific experience of sexism and racism from white male reporters and those in charge of the match. At first they would not let me in because they didn't believe I was a reporter, then after I produced my press card they allowed me in but throughout the afternoon they made racist and sexist jokes against me.

Black women journalists, like white women, are supposed only to write about food, children and so-called 'black stories'. Rianna Scipio, ex-weather presenter, was trained by the BBC as a presenter/researcher but ended up presenting the weather at weekends for LWT. She made it clear that: 'Basically I am a presenter who reads the weather. It's not as if I have a passion for the subject but, like an actress, you take whatever part comes up'. (The *Journal* 29/9/94)

Black women in the media who want to produce serious programmes on television find it difficult to do so despite their experience and training. Many of the white men who run the stations believe that, as one journalist put it, 'black women should not be in television reporting'. These men would feel more comfortable 'if all black women in television were working in the canteen'.

Black women journalists are rarely considered for senior positions and spend years working in junior positions without any prospect of advancement. One told me that when she applied for a senior job in television, she was told that she should be 'grateful to have a job at all'. A provincial newspaper journalist applied for the deputy-editor's position and was told that 'male journalists would not take orders from her', although she was already doing the deputy-editor's job when he was away.

Another woman journalist who had worked for six years in a mainstream magazine was overlooked twice when the deputy editor's job came up. When she asked why, she was told that she hadn't the experience. Yet the job was given to a man who had considerably less experience. She rightly left the magazine soon after. And another was not just overlooked for promotion but was expected to train the white man who was going to take over her job. She said:

> I worked as a producer for a community radio station for two years and suddenly management brought in a young white man to take over my job. He had just graduated from Oxford and did not know anything about radio producing and they expected me to teach him. I refused. The reason why he was brought in was because the programme had become popular and they felt that they no longer wanted a black woman to run things. The problem was that the programme was for black listeners and neither management nor this man knew or cared what the black community wanted to listen to. I left and the programme ceased to cater for the black community.

Black women, like white women who work in the media, are also likely to have no children or to delay motherhood. Many black women journalists I spoke to are aware of the pressures upon family life. A television reporter told me resignedly:

> I have two children and had to leave my husband because he refused to look after the children at night when I had to work. He also wanted me to leave my job and stay home to look after the children because he was jealous of my success. I was earning more than he.

Another said:

> I have one child but my boyfriend refused to help look after her because he said it's my job not his, so I had to find some-one to look after her when I am working late. I had to give up a good job because I couldn't find a childminder who would look after my children at odd hours. Now I am doing freelance work until she is older.

However, most black women journalists I spoke to had no children although they were aged between 25 and 35. As they said: 'I hope to get married and have a family but I need first to work out how the child is going to be cared for while I am at work.' 'I wouldn't dream of having children until I have built up my career on a sound footing'. Others do not want children because 'it would be bad for my career. If I take time off to have children I will have to start at the bottom and I might not even be able to get back into journalism.'

Black men find it difficult to accept that black women are achieving in greater numbers than they are in both education and jobs. Ann-Marie Baptiste argues that 'there is an ambition gap' developing between black women and men. Black males, she says, hate the idea that 'black women are trying harder and gaining more success and that this cuts through the heart of Black Manhood' (*Daily Express,* 9/3/95).

Because of their relative success and black men's fear of it, black women find it difficult to establish lasting relationships with black men. There is already controversy, especially among black women, over successful black men, who take white partners to show that they have made it. Of course, there are many famous black men who doubtless are motivated by love but what is difficult to understand is why they love only white women, especially when they were brought up, often single-handedly, by black mothers to whom they owe their lives.

Successful black women in the media

A number of black women have achieved success in the media, some more prominently than others. Women such as Zeynab Badawi have been presenting television news for years and have influenced a whole generation of black women. A television journalist declared:

> Moira Stewart was my role model because she was the only black woman on television and just seeing her there made me realised it was possible for black women to work on television.

One journalist said, 'I would like to think that my success was due to hard work and being good at the job I do.' A black woman deputy-editor of a local newspaper – rare for a woman, let alone a black woman – admitted that she experienced racism and sexism but this did not stop her from getting to the top. A senior radio producer voiced the same sentiment saying, 'If black people don't succeed they should not blame racism but themselves. I experienced discrimination but that did not stop me from achieving'. There are even some black women journalists who told me that they never experienced racism or sexism.

However, success should not be judged only by having a staff job in national papers, television, or radio stations, although this is what black people should be seeking when they become journalists. There are also hundreds of specialised publications and free newspapers to which black journalists can offer articles and eventually apply for jobs when they come up. Black journalists with training and experience can do freelance journalism, which can be interesting and rewarding although the pay and conditions are less good.

What has been established is that black women journalists who have succeeded generally do not let discrimination get in their way. Ability and determination are important for success but, as we have seen, getting into the media and achieving depends also on being in the right place at the right time. It is clear, however, that black people will have to campaign for change if they are to gain better representation in training and jobs in the media, and that women and men will have to work with and not against one another.

CHAPTER 6

MEDIA UNIONS AND BLACK PEOPLE

'It's no good trade unions only talking about equal opportunities, talk has to be translated into action'. (TUC, 1987)

Unions: an historical overview

The actions of trade unions, particularly in the 1960s, reflected the racism of British society. The unions did nothing to stop black workers being recruited to only the lowest paid jobs and when there was a recession the unions' motto was 'last in, first out' and this disproportionely affected the black workers. Reports by Daniels (1967), Rose et al (1969) and Smith (1977) showed that black workers faced massive discrimination at work and many were unemployed yet the unions did little to prevent this. Smith (1977) observed that such a situation could not have existed without racial discrimination being practised by the unions.

Things only began to change as a result of the 1975 Sex Discrimination Act and the 1976 Race Relations Act. Unions were forced to take these Acts seriously because they were law and because more women and black people were becoming union members. Colin Brown's 1984 survey found that in post-war Britain black immigrants and their children were joining unions in greater numbers than white workers. More black people were in organised work places such as public transport, hospitals and local government services. Brown found that 57 per cent of white men were in unions compared with 61 per cent of black men and that more black women than white were union members. But even the black members did not believe that the unions wanted to oppose or were opposing racism in the workplace. *Racism Within Trade Unions* (1984) states that:

> Despite policy documents, resolutions, race relations courses, conferences and public statements by the TUC and unions, blacks,

particularly the young, are still distrustful of the trade union movement. They believe that the unions have no firm intention of realis-
ing those policies where it matters most, opposing racism in the
workplace. (1984, 5)

Black members distrust unions because they see little evidence in union
structures to indicate that unions are serious about equal opportunity. For
example, unions employ very few black people as local or national full-
time officials and union officials refuse to attend race relations courses
because they think it unnecessary, yet their actions are often discriminatory.

The appointment of Bill Morris as General Secretary of the Transport
and General Workers Union in 1991 was a positive step for the trade
union movement. He was the first black person to be national leader of
a union in post-war Britain. He is seen as a role model: his appointment
shows that, given the opportunity, black people can achieve high
leadership inside and outside trade unions. However, this should not
obscure the fact that there are still too few black people employed as
officers. The situation was such that in 1987 the Trades Union Congress
(TUC) was forced to issue a *Black Workers'* Charter in response to the
gross under-representation of black trade union representatives on public
bodies, both local and national. The TUC asked unions to 'make efforts
to ensure that black members are nominated to such bodies whenever
possible' (1987).

The issue of racism within the workplace and racism suffered by black
members at the hands of white members has always been difficult for
unions. The TUC *Charter* advises unions to make firm policies and take
action to eradicate racism from the workplace. It also recommends that
unions educate their members against racist 'myths' and 'propaganda'
against black people and instead encourage white members to see the
'positive' contribution that black workers are making to industry and the
unions. These policies, the TUC hoped, will be accepted by unions and
management.

The 1991 TUC report *Involvement of Ethnic Minority Workers* shows
just how difficult it is for trade unions to get to grips with black inequality since trade unions were still failing to meet the needs of their
black workers. The 1991 report found that unions were often ineffective

in defending black members in racial discrimination cases. Unions were not carrying out ethnic monitoring or adopting an overall bargaining strategy for race equality.

According to the 1994 *Labour Force Survey*, black workers make up 5.9 per cent of the working population but three times as many black people are unemployed as whites and a disproportionate number are concentrated in low-paid jobs.

Clearly, the unions are still failing to represent black members in negotiations, especially when management target black workers for redundancy because of their colour. The TUC has set out guidelines for unions on how to deal with redundancy, ensuring that no one sex or race is predominantly affected. The last in, first out policy still affects black workers, however, especially if they were recruited during a positive action programme. The TUC advises that personnel be told that it is unacceptable for decisions about who is to be made redundant to be taken on the grounds of gender or race.

The difficulties many unions face with inequality stems from the fact that many union members do not believe that women or black people should have equality or that such issues should be part of unions' negotiating strategy. They find it difficult to understand that better wages and working conditions, which are at the heart of trade unionism, also means giving women and black people equal opportunities. The TUC, in its effort to make equal opportunities an important issue for the union movement, has taken steps to change its own structure and to give more say to black union members. In 1991 it passed a motion to give black people seats on the General Council and its committees. It took three years before this motion was put into action and three seats were set aside for black representatives on the TUC General Council, including one for a black woman. A Race Relations Committee was set up in 1994 and four additional seats were created in 1995 on the TUC Women's Committee for black women.

After setting an example, the TUC has called upon affiliated unions to carry out similar policies to improve black representation in unions' decision-making policies and to tackle discrimination in the workplace. So far most unions have not changed significantly. But the presence of more black representatives within the TUC and the positive action of this body towards equality could in the end ensure that all unions make equality an integral part of their work.

The National Union of Journalists

The National Union of Journalists is said to be the largest journalists' union in the world. It has 25,000 members, down from 32,000 in the mid-'80s. This reduction in membership is mainly due to the loss of journalists and editorial staff in the media, coupled with the imposition of short-term and individual contracts. There are other media unions which represent journalists and editorial staff, including the Institute of Journalists, with less than 2,000 members, and the Broadcasting and Entertainment Cinematograph Television Union (BECTU), which represents less than 1,000 journalists working in broadcasting.

The NUJ was established in 1907 at a conference in Birmingham. At the time equality was not an issue; it was not even considered. Women journalists were too few to count and there were no black journalists at the meeting and very few in Britain at the time. Clement Bundock recorded that:

> the conference was an event of deep significance in the history of journalism and journalists in the British Isles. With no danger of exaggeration it may be said to have begun a revolution in the conditions under which journalists do their work particularly in the payment they receive for the work they do. (1957, 8)

The history of the NUJ shows how influential the Union has been in the fight for better wages and working conditions for journalists. Before 1957 the wages, working conditions and training of journalists were minimal and most journalists were paid the same as a junior clerk and their education was as poor. Journalism students were only expected to have the three Rs. Before the NUJ was set up, a group of journalists calling themselves the Working Journalists of the United Kingdom expressed the strong conviction that a new organisation should be established, capable of safeguarding and furthering the interest of working journalists, and suggested that it be called the National Union of Journalists. They declared that:

> The union should be opened to all journalists (not newspaper proprietors, managers or directors) who are or have been for three years

regularly engaged in the profession, and its objects should be to defend their professional interest by taking action to remove definite grievances with regard to salaries, conditions of employment and tenure of office; to establish out of work benevolent and super-annuation funds; and to deal with questions affecting professional conduct and etiquette. (1957, 10)

Over the last 90 years the NUJ has defended the wages and working conditions of journalists and those doing other editorial work. The high status and relatively high wages of some journalists has made the occupation very popular, so much so that half of all graduates in Britain want to work in the media (*Furthering Education*, 1995). However, because of the changes in the industry and the de-recognition of the Union by many media employers, the NUJ's position has weakened in recent years.

In the area of training the NUJ has been, and still is, a part of the National Council for the Training of Journalists (NCTJ) since it was formed in 1957. The Union has played an important role in deciding what educational qualifications were needed for journalism training. Educational qualifications for journalism students were raised and the Union also had a say in who entered newspaper journalism. Critics argue that the NCTJ and the NUJ had too much power over newspaper journalists' training (Boyd-Barrett, 1980) but in the 1980s, the NCTJ lost its power and the monopoly on newspaper journalism training. This was partly because National Vocational Qualifications (NVQs) were brought in which allowed colleges and newspapers to provide training without accreditation from the NCTJ.

The NUJ and Equal Opportunities

Because the NUJ represents most journalists in Britain its structure and its equal opportunities policies merit scrutiny. The Union represents journalists in every sector of the media and has expanded since its establishment in 1907 for newspaper journalists only. Every member can belong to a chapel at work and a branch, which covers where the chapel is located. The day-to-day running of the geographical area is done by area councils and delegates are elected to these by the branches. The NUJ has seven industrial councils covering national and provincial newspapers, broadcasting, public relations, books, magazines and freelance work. These industrial councils are responsible for promoting and negotiating wages and conditions with employers and individuals on matters affecting members within their sector.

In 1986 the NUJ issued an equal opportunities statement as part of its agreement with the TUC guidelines on equality. It states:

The NUJ is an equal opportunities employer. The aim of our policy is to ensure that no job applicant or employee receives less favourable treatment on the grounds of race, colour, nationality, ethnic or national origin, religious beliefs, sex, marital status, gender, sexual orientation, or is disadvantaged by conditions or requirements which cannot be shown to be justifiable. There will be no discrimination against persons with disabilities who have the necessary attributes for a post. Selection criteria and procedures will be frequently reveiwed to ensure that individuals are selected, promoted and treated on the basis of their relevant merits and abilities. All employees will be given equal opportunities and where appropriate special training to progress within the organisation. The union is committed to a programme of positive action to make this policy fully effective as set out in our objectives of the union. The union will also observe the letter and spirit of the Rehabilitation of Offenders Act.

This was a positive step for the Union to have taken in 1986 but concern for equality went back to the 1970s. Race equality policies began with the forming of the Union's Race Relations Working Party (RRWP). This committee lasted 16 years, until replaced by the Black Members' Council (BMC) in 1990. The RRWP was very active in its time. It began by campaigning against racist reporting but by the 1980s it had broadened its campaign to include the under-representation of black people in journalism training and jobs. It also argued for ethnic monitoring within the NUJ, as recommended from by the TUC to the unions.

Before ethnic monitoring the NUJ had no idea how many of its members were black or women. The Working Party proposal was to change this but a significant number of members were against ethnic monitoring. They argued that it was 'apartheid' and that ir was 'belittling' to give information on their ethnic origin: Some maintained that: 'We don't need such questions; we have an equal opportunities policy', and 'It's the bosses who should be putting this question on their job applications; it is they who are prejudiced'.

What was significant was the fury created in the Union by so simple a request and the fear of so many about knowing how few black members there were. Perhaps they feared that the information would oblige the Union to take action against racism in the media. Ethnic monitoring provides evidence that not only is an organisation or union discriminatory but also that Britain is a racist country – and few want to admit this.

Despite the objections, the NUJ put ethnic monitoring of new members into place and it is still in force today. The Union is now able to get annual updates of its ethnic minority members. In 1996 only 1.6 per cent of its members were black, less than a third of the national black British population percentage. Clearly, the NUJ's policy on getting more black people into journalism is still failing despite all their public statements on equal opportunities.

Race conferences and editors

As part of its campaign against racism in the media, the RRWP held several regional conferences and seminars in partnership with the CRE during the 1980s. The Working Party saw these gatherings as vital to press the media to train and employ more black journalists and also to improve the reporting on issues of race. The NUJ's *Guidelines On Race Reporting* states:

1   Only mention someone's race if it is strictly relevant. Check to make sure you have it right. Would you mention race if the person was white?

2   Do not sensationalise race relations issues; it harms black people and it could harm you. Think carefully about the words you use. Words which were once in common usage are now considered offensive, e.g. half-caste and coloured. Use mixed-race and black instead. Black can cover people of Arab, Asian, Chinese and African origin. Ask people how they define themselves.

3   Immigrant is often used as a term of abuse. Do not use it unless the person really is an immigrant. Most black people in Britain were born here and most immigrants are white.

4   Do not make assumptions about a person's cultural background –
    whether it is their name or religious detail. Ask them, or where this
    is not possible check with the local community relations council.

5   Investigate the treatment of black people in education, health,
    employment and housing. Do not forget travellers and gypsies.
    Cover their lives and concerns. Seek the views of their repre-
    sentatives.

6   Remember that black communities are culturally diverse. Get a full
    and correct view from representative organisations.

7   Press for equal opportunities for employment of black staff. Be wary
    of discrimination. Just because a source is traditional does not mean
    it is accurate.

REPORTING RACIST ORGANISATIONS

8   When interviewing representatives of racist organisations or report-
    ing meetings or statements or claims, journalists should carefully
    check all reports for accuracy and seek rebutting or opposing
    comments. The anti-social nature of such views should be exposed.

9   Do not sensationalise by reports, photographs, film or presentation,
    the activities of racist organisations. Seek to publish or broadcast
    material exposing the myths and lies of racist organisations and their
    anti-social behaviour.

10 Do not allow the letters column or 'phone in' programmes to be
    used to spread racial hatred in whatever guise.

The above guidelines were often flouted by NUJ members in national
tabloids, local and provincial newspapers and were an important topic
for discussion. As a member of the RRWP for five years and its chair for
two years, I attended all the conferences on race from 1986 till 1990.
Local editors, journalists and people from the black community were
invited to conferences held outside London. Most editors did not accept
our invitation but those who did gave us a clear picture of how the media
operated. Despite the evidence, editors often failed to see that many of
the stories they published concerning race were pejoratively biased.

When we asked why local papers trained or employed none or so few
black people, we received the same tired excuse that black people don't

apply. One editor of a West Midlands newspaper, when asked why he did not advertise jobs and training places in black newspapers, answered angrily that if 'coloured people can't be bothered to look in my paper I won't be putting ads. in any other paper'. This editor's contempt for black people was obvious so no wonder he had no black people on his newspaper.

Not all editors who attended these race conferences behaved like this but none ever admitted that their race reporting or employment practice was racist. Editors maintained that the media were 'objective' and that they themselves had a colour-blind attitude. At the end of these conferences promises were made to improve race reporting and the numbers of black people on journalists' training courses and jobs. But editors, I believe, were dishonest and used these conferences mainly as public relations exercises, with no intention of taking any action to redress the imbalance.

Black members' conferences

The RRWP held annual conferences in London, supported by the NUJ's National Executive as part of its equal opportunities policy. These conferences were well attended by black members of the Union. White members were welcome to attend but few ever did. One told me that racism was a 'black problem' and so should be left to black people. Such views, although dated, are held by many in the NUJ and in society, which is why they have never taken equal opportunities very seriously.

The conferences sought to examine the under-representation of black people in journalism training and jobs, how the situation could be changed and the role of the NUJ. The training workshops were usually over-subscribed and it soon became clear to members of the RRWP that journalism training was the key to jobs. We found too that very few black people were getting training. Delegates described their experience and discussed individual journalism courses' attitude towards black applicants.

Few displayed the positive approaches of, for example, City University in London, which asked applicants for photographs and made sure that they interviewed all black applicants and that ten percent of their journalism students were black. What we discovered at these conferences was that if you are black, high educational qualifications do not necessarily get you an interview for a place on a recognised journalism course. The consensus was that because of racism, most journalism courses took only a token few black people. We found, however, that journalism courses were much more generous about women: taking 40 per cent of women but less than one per cent of black people.

The contents of courses were also criticised because they fail to recognise or mention racism and race reporting. However, most did recognise and mention sex discrimination. One delegate talked about the journalism course he attended, reporting that 'There was an absolute refusal to discuss the question of political visibility of black people in relation to the establishment'.

Black members did not agree with the commonly held assumption that black people did not apply for training, because they were proof that black people did. Some members argued that there should be quotas which would force journalism courses to take on more black students, while others argued against it as against the law in Britain. In the United States, where quotas were used from the 1970s until the Reagan administration put a halt to them, whites began to use the law to challenge quotas, claiming that it was reverse discrimination.

It was also suggested that more black tutors be employed on courses. There are two problems with this idea. Firstly, the hiring of more black tutors will not necessarily increase the numbers of black students. It is not the black tutors but management who make the decisions on admissions. Secondly, there are very few black journalists at present with the experience needed to teach journalism students. Monitoring and targeting are better solutions but very few courses monitor and none at present does targeting.

On the subject of higher education, black members did not want a lowering of educational qualifications for black people to enter journalism training because most delegates were graduates and did not need this concession. And as one delegate argued, 'if standards were lowered for black people we would not be seen as equal' and this would affect black people's access to jobs.

We concluded that there should be an attack on the education system and its low expectations of black pupils. Delegates also believed that the

NUJ has a vital role which they are not fulfilling and that the NUJ should organise short-term courses for black people and negotiate with mainstream courses to undertake monitoring and targeting. Although the NUJ has sponsored black students for media courses since 1987 through its George Viner Fund, it has never run a black-only journalism course. This, I believe, would help give journalistic skills to more black people.

Workshops on employment

Workshops on employment were also well attended at the Race Relations Working Party conferences. Black members agreed that the media's equal opportunities policies were only 'window dressing' and that employers hid behind the stated equal opportunities policies to avoid taking actions that might precipitate change.

The NUJ was constantly criticised by black members for their reluctance in helping black journalists to get jobs. At the Union's 1986 Annual Delegate Meeting (ADM) a resolution was passed instructing industrial councils to have an equal opportunities clause in their house agreements, which would encourage the employment of more black journalists through measures such as monitoring and targeting. But so far these councils have largely ignored negotiating on race equality: women, however, have fared better.

As chair of the RRWP in 1987, I met with representatives of the Union's industrial councils and tried to persuade them to include black equality in their house agreements. My impression was that these men would have preferred not to meet me. They moved about uncomfortably when discussing race equality. One told me that, while he agreed that there were very few black people in media jobs and was sympathetic, he did not think that 'management or staff would accept monitoring and targeting'. Targeting would mean fewer jobs for white journalists and neither management nor white staff would agreed to this. Representatives from the Union's industrial councils saw targeting as reverse discrimination and I could not convince them that ethnic monitoring and targeting would help to redress the balance.

Black members at conference examined the Union's record of employment and found that the Union has never had a full-time black official, although for a short time in the 1990s it employed a black man as head of its accountancy department. Delegates felt that it was hypo-critical for the NUJ to ask management to employ more black journalists when the Union itself still did not employ a single black full-time official, and that the NUJ should get 'its own house in order before it can ask management to change'.

The NUJ's failure to put equal opportunities into practice is due to the differences between Union leaders and white members. While those who run the Union will at least publicly agree to positive actions, the general membership is unenthusiastic. Although equal opportunities policies are voted in at the Union's AGM by political activists, the problem arises when these polices are to be put into practice and the rest of the members disagree. Quite simply, racism does not affect over 98 per cent of the Union members directly and so most cannot or will not understand its effects on black people.

The 1986 RRWP conference on print journalism recommended that the NUJ kept close contact with and put pressure on media employers to take on more black journalists. The conference also called for the NUJ to ap-point an Equal Opportunities Officer to deal with all aspects of equality and negotiate for the Union with employers like the BBC. However, the main recommendation from the 1986 conference was that the Union should increase the membership of the RRWP above the existing seven. The Union was also asked to 'increase its funds and other facilities' to the RRWP so as to tackle racism in the media more effectively.

The 1988 RRWP conference, entitled Black People and the NUJ, acknowledged that black equality remains a problem for the NUJ despite the RRWP's attempts. In his opening address the Chair of RRWP had this to say:

I don't think that the NUJ as a whole takes the issue of race equality seriously. It is regarded as a marginal issue, which should be left safely in the hands of the Race Relations Working Party. Race equality issues do not permeate through the organisation and struc-ture of the Union. How many black members are in the NUJ? Why are there so few and what are the causes? Ask these questions and you will get all sorts of answers except the one that points the finger directly at the racism which is present both in the Union and in the profession as a whole. How can the Union be structured to make it more acceptable and relevant to potential black members? These are the questions which need serious answers if the NUJ is to mean anything to black journalists. (1988, 20)

The view that the NUJ was not taking race equality seriously was echoed throughout the day in the workshops. Conference agreed that the NUJ must consider and come to terms with three overlapping and interrelated issues: black members within the NUJ and trade union movement, black employees and their representation in the workplace and the way the black community perceived the NUJ. Issues affecting black members were discussed, including NUJ structures, training, employment and the black press.

Black members were clear that equal opportunity policies were not being pursued by the Union because it feared losing white members who would object. On training, similar views were expressed to those in former conferences but generally it was agreed that the Union should continue to put pressure on media organisations to take on more black people on training courses. Conference welcomed the George Viner Memorial Fund which sponsored black people on media courses and called for the Union to sponsor short courses for black people – a recommendation made at previous conferences but still not realised.

On employment, the conference repeated its call on the NUJ to increase pressure on media managers to employ more black journalists. Conference concluded that the most effective means to carry out these proposals was to set up a black section within the NUJ. This proposal was taken to the NUJ's annual delegate meeting in 1990 and was accepted. The Black Members' Council (BMC) replaced the RRWP.

The Black Members' Council

The council was to be made up of 12 members: five elected by black NUJ members and one from each of the Union's industrial councils plus one member from the Scottish and Irish Councils. All should in principle be black. Like the RRWP, the BMC's long-term aims were to increase the numbers of black people in journalism courses and jobs and to campaign generally against racism in the media and society. In theory, the BMC should have more members and more funds to help it carry out its aim in redressing the balance in the media but it does not.

The BMC has had limited success since its creation and its critics believe it has had none. It was set up in a spirit of hopefulness and optimism but at the time of writing it is facing turmoil because of individual differences. Unable to attract black members, it has only half the number it needs to carry out its work. There seem to be several reasons for the lack of support from black members. One is that Council does not communicate sufficiently with black members in the Union – probably because of its small budget. Secondly, as I have argued in Chapter One, most black journalists who are working on staff are reluctant to join a campaigning body like the BMC fearing that they might be sacked if employers find out. So they do not get involved although they might agree with the principle.

But the fundamental problem is that the NUJ does not place race equality high on its agenda and its funds to the BMC are negligible, inadequate for the Council to carry out its work properly. Because the NUJ has scant evidence that it is serious about race equality, black members have no confidence that the BMC can change the Union. Over the years since the Union issued its equal opportunities statement, the only real evidence of action is the George Viner Fund: other proposals have been left on the shelves or binned. The NUJ's position on equal opportunities is indicated by the response in 1990 to financial difficulties. One of its first actions was to get rid of its Equal Opportunities Officer after only three years, moving her to another job in the Union and scrapping the equal opportunities post. The Union said it could not afford it.

Despite its problems, the BMC has struggled on with its campaign against racism in the media and society. It has joined the International Federation of Journalists Media Group helping to campaign against racism and xenophobia in Europe. It has plans to gather information on the numbers of black journalists working in national newspapers – information they hope to use when they approach media management about the gross under-representation of black people in the media (AGM, 1998).

In 1996, the BMC was involved in organising a successful European journalists' conference on race held in London called White Voices, White Faces, White Views which brought together journalists and experts on training and recruitment from all over Europe. The conference recommended that funds be provided by central government, employers and charitable trusts for the sponsorship of black students onto journalism courses and that there should be 'employment targets' for black people in the media. Black tutors of journalism should be employed and ethnic monitoring carried out at journalism colleges and at the workplace. These recommendations will, I believe, have the support of most black journalists and could be used as a foundation for change. But will government or media employers be prepared to take up these recommendations and, crucially, will black journalists be prepared to join the BMC and put in the time and effort needed to achieve race equality?

The Equality Council

As part of its equal opportunities policies in the 1970s, the NUJ created the Equality Council just as it did the RRWP, in response to the growing call for equal opportunities and the new legislation. However, it was obvious from the start that gender equality had more support in the Union than race. The Equality Council in the 1980s had more money, more members and more influence than the RRWP. It is also fair to say that this Council was better organised and its members worked very hard on educating Union members as well as the media industry about sexism in the media. Their leaflets and booklets, such as the *Equality Style Guide* and *Images of Women,* helped to promote gender equality through journalism. The *Equality Style Guide* gave advice on appropriate words and phrases for journalists to use that do not discriminate against women. The Council deals mainly with gender equality, although their work also involves disability and gay and lesbian rights.

There is a stark difference between gender and race equality in the NUJ and other unions. Giving women equality is far more acceptable than giving equality to black people. We have seen that 40 per cent of NUJ members are female compared with 1.6 per cent black. Women make up 50 per cent of journalism students and 55 per cent in some colleges, whereas on most mainstream journalism courses black students make up less than 1 per cent. The NUJ has eleven full-time officials: not one is black, three are women, although a black woman came a close second in a recent election for deputy general secretary.

When most employers and unions think of equality they do so only in terms of gender equality because it is easier to give white middle-class women equality. Working-class and black women are generally left out. Black women journalists are still far in the minority compared to white women.

The Ethics Council

The NUJ Ethics Council, set up in 1987, was seen as another step in the Union's equal opportunities policy. This Council is to promote and enforce the Union's Code of Conduct which forms part of the Union rule book by which members are bound. In theory, members can be disciplined if they breach the code which lays down, among other things, the rules relating to race and gender reporting by NUJ members. In its 1987 publication, *Media Standards*, the NUJ explained that the Ethics Council aimed to promote the Code through education but that anyone in the public who objects to what they see hear or read in the media can complain directly to the Ethics Council, which would seek to resolve the complaint:

The Ethics Council will seek redress through, for example, the right of reply, an apology and/or correction or an agreement to prevent recurrence of the breach. Wherever, possible, the Ethics Council will deal with complaints as a collective issue by involving the journalists' chapel. The Ethics Council's duties are to promote the NUJ's Code of Conduct among the general public and high ethical standards among NUJ journalists, to publicise breaches of the Code both inside and outside the union and to enlist the support from other news media unions. The council can and does receive complaints from NUJ branches and individual members and from members of the public about the work and behaviour of NUJ members. However the Ethics Council does not deal with complaints involving advertisement as those responsible are not NUJ members. It also cannot force those who run the media to put right a breach of ethical standards; that would require legislation. (1987)

After nine years of the Ethics Council and hundreds of complaints, very few members found guilty of breaching the Union's Code of Conduct were fined. So far, one journalist has been fined and dismissed from the Union because he refused to pay the fine. Threats of fines and dismissal never stopped racist reporting, so strong was the need by some national tabloids to keep negating black people. Instead, the Council's work was criticised for being harsh on its own members. Consequently at the Union's 1991 ADM, the following proposal was agreed:

That ADM recognises that the disciplinary approach to ethics has failed for many reasons and that the enforcement of the Code of Conduct is primarily a collective responsibility, in particular a matter of education and of chapels pressing editors and proprietors to adopt policies favourable to the implementation of the code as opposed to policies which encourage journalists to break it. ADM instructs the NEC to remind chapels and members that the code of conduct is part of the union's rules. ADM nevertheless recognises that there will be certain occasions when a journalist's behaviour is so bad that the NUJ will want publicly to disassociate itself and that in such cases a rule 22 procedure would still be appropriate. ADM therefore instructs the NEC as a matter of urgency to amend the rules in order that the Ethics Council shall deal with education and propaganda on ethical matters while the Ethics Council shall still be empowered to receive complaints from members of the public. Its role shall be restricted to inquiring into and making comments about those matters if it deems it helpful to the union's overall work of promoting the code.

The passing of this motion ensured that the NUJ abandoned its policy to discipline members who flout its code of conduct. The Ethics Council is said to have lost its teeth, if it ever had any. Now that its role has been reduced to the safe area of education, journalists can go back to racist and sexist reporting without fear lest they flout the Union's code of conduct.

The commonsense view was that too many NUJ members were breaking the Code of Conduct for it to be possible to discipline them all. The NUJ would lose hundreds of members and their subscriptions, just when membership was down and finances severely depleted. Basically, objectors to the Ethics Council are admitting that the Union is powerless to stop racist and sexist reporting and portrayals by its members.

The reduction of the Ethics Council's power was not well received by black union members and the black community as a whole. One journalist I interviewed remarked:

I did not think that the Ethics Council was very powerful but at least they could discipline members who write rubbish about us, but now they are even allowed to do this.

Another said:

The NUJ is powerless against racist and sexist reporting and this proves it. I am not surprised the NUJ won't do anything against its white members to help us blacks. It's sad that the Union has done this. The Ethics Council should be able to level severe penalties against those who write such stories but the Union won't do much for its black members when money is involved. As soon as there is a problem equality policies are cut.

Broadcast Unions

Before its amalgamation with BETA in 1991, the Association of Cinematograph Television and Allied Technicians (ACTT) outlined its equal opportunities policies in a 1988 *Code of Practice on Racism*. The Union stated it was:

strategically placed to intervene against racism both in terms of media content and also in terms of job opportunities in films, television and other areas where the Union organises.

ACTT identified two main areas of concern: the under-representation of black members and the 'racist images and assumptions which proliferate on our screens' (ACTT, 1984, 1). The code called on ACTT members not to work on material that incites racial hatred or stereotyping. It called on members working in news and current affairs to ensure that coverage of the black community is fair and accurate. In particular, members should make sure that a person's race or colour be mentioned only when strictly relevant to the story. If racist allegations are made or racist views expressed, black and anti-racist organisations should have an automatic right of reply. Sympathetic presentations of racism and racist ideas should be discouraged.

The ACTT Code asked members to press for equal opportunities for all people regardless of race and colour. Members involved in recruitment and promotion they should ensure that the procedures involved follow good equal opportunities practice, for instance placing job advertise-

ments in the ethnic press. Members working in drama and light entertainment should, if it is in their power to do so, ensure that black actors
and actresses are considered for all roles on the basis of ability not race.

In addition to their code of practice issued to members together with
their TUC agreement, ACTT made a number of policy decisions on race.
In their report *Ten Years of ACTT Equality Policies*, a list of proposals
and resolutions on equality at yearly conferences gave a picture of how
ACTT conference reacted to equal opportunities policies throughout the
1980s. In 1982 ACTT appointed its first Equal Opportunities Officer.
One proposal at the 1982 conference was for consideration to be given
to positive action for women and ethnic groups in respect of Union
membership. This was turned down by delegates. However, they voted
for four seats on the equality committee to be reserved for black
members. In 1984 ACTT conference welcomed the sub-committee on
racial equality but refused to strengthen the Code of Practice on race. In
1985 another proposal for updating the Code on racism was defeated.
This proposal was not only that the race Code be strengthened but that
equality officers and shop stewards attend racism awareness courses
(ACTT, 1988).

At the time ACTT had 18 full-time officers and, like the NUJ, none was
black. In 1991 ACTT merged with BECTA, a Union representing
journalists and broadcasters in television and radio. The new Union,
BECTU, has 18 full-time officers but only one is black. It might be that
one is better than none but it does not show much change in the Union's
position on race equality after 15 years. The under-representation of
black people as full-time officials in the NUJ and BECTU is not because
well-qualified black people did not apply but because the selection
process went against them.

ACTT's Equal Opportunities Officer in 1989 told me that the vacancy
for the equal opportunities post was advertised in the ethnic press as is
the policy of the Union. Seventeen of the 65 applicants were black but
during the selection process only two black men – and no black women
– were given a second interview although some were considered to be
good. She explained that this was because those interviewing did not
have anti-racist training and did not follow the procedure, and said that
many trade union officers rejected anti-racist training because they did

not think that they needed it. Another problem according to the then Equal Opportunities Officer, was that so few black people applied to join ACTT. She thought that one reason was that four members were required to sponsor them. After complaints, the Union stopped this practice, deciding instead on a membership committee.

Involvement with the training scheme *JOBFIT* was one of the positive achievements of ACTT's equal opportunities policies. This Joint Board for Film Industry Training was set up in1985 by ACTT, the British Film and Television Producers Association (BFTPA) and the Independent Programme Producers Association (IPPA). The Advertising Film and Video Producers Association (AFVPA) and Channel 4 became sponsors of the scheme in 1986. *JOBFIT* is the first systematic industry-wide training scheme in the freelance film-making sector. *JOBFIT* has now been re-named *FT2* but its work has not changed.

Trainees are attached to various film production companies over a two-year period. They are taken into the scheme in groups of 12, at intervals compatible with production cycles. On satisfactory completion of the two-year programme, trainees are eligible for ACTT membership and are then more likely to get employment in the industry. *JOBFIT/FT2* is committed to an equal opportunities policy and strongly encourages and supports applications from women and ethnic minorities. The training scheme is financed on an industry-wide level by all film production made under agreements between the Employers' Association and the ACTT.

BECTU Black Members' Conference

After the amalgamation of ACTT and BETA in 1991, a conference was called by black members of both Unions to discuss the new Union's (Broadcast Entertainment Cinematograph and Theatre Union, BECTU) position on equal opportunities. The conference, *Black To The Future,* dealt with training, employment, monitoring, and media racism inside and outside the Union. The conference urged officials of the joint Union to address the issue of a black members' forum whereby black members could have a voice. Like the NUJ Black Members Council, black members in BECTU criticised Union structures for not being 'accessible to black people' (BECTU, 1991, 2). On the issue of employment, the conference recommended that BECTU build a profile of companies who were not interviewing/employing black freelances. It was felt that the equality laws should change and that what was needed was a law similar to that in Northern Ireland which gave Catholics increased opportunities in employment.

Conference also called for a form of contract compliance to be adopted so that the BBC and Independent Television can give work only to independent television companies who implement equal opportunities. It also urged that commercial companies be challenged with figures showing that black people form a significant part of their viewing audience, asserting that in London nearly 40 per cent of people under 25 who watched *London Weekend Television* were black. The conference condemned word of mouth recruitment, pointing out its unfairness to black people.

The media unions think they have moved a long way towards equality but they still have a long way to go before they genuinely fulfill their obligations. Too few black people are in full-time official posts and they marginalise the issue of racism to race councils instead of making it a union priority.

The value of unions for black journalists

Many black journalists I spoke to argued that media unions, especially the NUJ, are powerless to stop racist reporting and the under-representation of black people in the media even if they wanted to. The following comments are typical:

> Unions can't do much to stop racism. They probably could through their closed shop but now their influence is dwindling.

> Newspaper proprietors are much more powerful and they take little notice of unions who are losing their power.

> Unions are not effective agents for change. They cannot influence employers to take on more ethnic minorities.

> It depends on management being convinced that equal opportunities are important.

On the subject of jobs, some black members told me that black people should not expect media unions to get them training and jobs because 'If blacks are good enough they will get in without any help from the unions. No newspaper will turn you down because you are a black if you have a good story.' Another said: 'If the climate is right and you are good at what you do you get in'.

Despite the general criticism, some black journalists have had positive experiences as members of media unions and believe that although the unions should be doing more, being a member is positive. As one newspaper journalist said:

> I have no idea what the media unions can do to get more black people into media jobs but I do know that being a member of the NUJ was good for me. They helped me when I was beaten up when I went to get a story. The Union supported me emotionally and legally. I can't praise them enough.

Another added:

> The Union does represent blacks and Asians to a certain extent but they should do more. They helped me fight for compensation and although I didn't get all I wanted they backed me financially and legally. It's not the Union, it's the people in it. If blacks stand up and fight for what they want they will get it.

A few others thought that the situation was changing sufficiently:

> It is difficult for unions but things are changing. Journalism is no longer a white male-dominated profession for there are some blacks and a number of women in the Union. It is up to black people to change the Union for their benefit.

Despite the failings of media unions on race equality, black members should continue to work for change through their unions. But it is not just the unions which need to put the struggle at the top of their agenda but black journalists too. Many black journalists are comfortable with the tokenist role. They are so grateful to get a job in mainstream journalism that they quickly 'put up and shut up'. Much still needs to be done. We should be committed to changing the *status quo* by education, agitation and organisation.

Bibliography

AINLEY, B. (1986) 'The Role of the NUJ's Race Relations Working Party' in NUJ *Print Journalism and Black People*, London: National Union of Journalists, pp. 8-10

AINLEY, B. (1994) *Blacks and Asians in the British Media*, PhD thesis, London University

AMERICAN NEWSPAPER PUBLISHERS' ASSOCIATION (1988) *Survey of Racial Minorities and Women in US Daily Newspapers*, Dallas, Texas: Belden Associates

ASSOCIATION OF CINEMATOGRAPH, TELEVISION AND ALLIED TECHNICIANS (1985) *Equality Code of Practice on Racism*, London: ACTT

BENJAMIN, I. (1995) *The Black Press in Britain*, Stoke on Trent: Trentham Books

BLACK MEDIA WORKERS' ASSOCIATION (1983) *Research Report No. 1*, London: BMWA

BOYD-BARRETT, O. (1970) 'Journalism Recruitment and Training: Problems in Professionalisation' in TUNSTALL, J. (ed) *Media Sociology*, London: Constable, pp. 181-201

BRAH, A. and DEEN, R. (1986) 'Towards anti-racist and anti-sexist schooling', *Critical Social Policy*, Vol. 6, No1, Summer

BRAHAM, P. (1982) 'How the Media Report Race' in GUREVITCH, M. *et al* (eds) *Culture, Society and the Media*, London: Methuen, pp. 268-286

BRAITHWAITE, E. (1967) in FRYER, P. *Staying Power*, London: Pluto Press

BRENNAN, J. and McGEEVOR, P. (1990) *Ethnic Minorities and the Graduate Labour Market*, London: Commission for Racial Equality

BRITISH BROADCASTING CORPORATION (1989) *News Trainees*, London: BBC Appointments

BRITISH FILM INSTITUTE (1994) *Television Industry Tracking Study*, London: BFI

BROADCASTING ENTERTAINMENT CINEMATOGRAPH THEATRE UNION (1991) *Black to the Future, Report on the Black Members' Conference*, London: BECTU

BROWN, C. (1984) *Black and White Britain: The Third PSI Survey*, London: Policy Studies Institute and Heinemann Educational Books

BRYANT, B., DADZIE, S. and SCAFE, S. (1985) *The Heart of the Race: Black Women's Lives in Britain,* London: Virago Press.

BUNDOCK, C. (1957) *The National Union of Journalists: A Jubilee History*, Oxford: NUJ.

CARDIFF CENTRE FOR JOURNALISM STUDIES, UNIVERSITY OF WALES (1991) *Postgraduate Diploma in Journalism Studies.*

CARBY, H. (1982) 'Schooling in Babylon' in THE CENTRE FOR CONTEMPORARY CULTURAL STUDIES *The Empire Strikes Back: Race and Racism in '70s Britain*, London: Hutchinson, pp. 183-211

CASHMORE, E. and TROYNA, B. (1983) *Introduction to Race Relations*, London: Routledge and Kegan Paul

CHANNER, Y. (1995) *I Am A Promise: The School Achievement Of British African Caribbeans*, Stoke on Trent: Trentham Books

CHEVANNES, M. and REEVES, F. (1987) 'The Black Voluntary School Movement: definition, context and prospects' in TROYNA, B. (ed) *Racial Inequality in Education*, London: Tavistock, pp. 147-169

CHRISTIAN, H. (1980) 'Journalists' Occupational Ideologies and Press Commercialisation', in CHRISTIAN, H. (ed) *The Sociology of Journalism and the Press*, Sociological Review Monograph 29, University of Keele. pp. 259-306

CITY UNIVERSITY (1991) *Post-Graduate Journalism Course*, London: City University Department of Journalism

COARD, B. (1971) *How the West Indian Child is made Educationally Subnormal in the British School System*, London: New Beacon Books

COLE, M. (1989) 'Monocultural, Multicultural and Anti-Racist Education' in COLE, M. (ed) *The Social Context of Schooling*, Lewes: Falmer Press. pp. 138-155

COLEMAN, J.S. *et al* (1969) *Equality of Educational Opportunity*, Cambridge, Mass: Harvard University Press

COMMONWEALTH IMMIGRANTS ADVISORY COUNCIL (1964) *Second Report*, London: HMSO, Cmnd. 2266

CRISPIN, C. (1977) *Ethnic Minorities in the Inner City*, London: Commission for Racial Equality

CRITCHER, C., PARKER, M. and RANJIT, S. (1975) *Race in the Provincial Press: A Case Study of Five West Midlands Newspapers*, Birmingham: Centre For Contemporary Cultural Studies, University of Birmingham

CROSS, M., WRENCH, J. and BARNETT, S. (1990) *Ethnic Minorities and the Careers Service*, University of Warwick Research Paper No. 73

CURTIN, P. (1965) *The Image Of Africa: British Ideas and Action 1780-1850*, London: Macmillan

DANIELS, W. (1968) *Racial Discrimination in England*, Harmondsworth: Penguin

DAVIES, K. *et al* (1987) *Out of Focus, Writings on Women and the Media*, London: The Women's Press 1987

DAY, M. (1988) 'Employment, Training and Equal Opportunities' in HARTE, J. (ed) *Black People and The Media; Equality in Employment and Training Policies and Practice*, London: CRE and London Borough of Lewisham, pp. 22-29

DAYES, S. (1987) The Black Middle Class, Birmingham: Aston University, unpublished PhD thesis

DELANO, A. and HENNINGHAM, J. (1995) *The News Breed: British Journalists in the 1990s*, London: London Institute

DEPARTMENT OF EDUCATION AND SCIENCE (1965) *The Education of Immigrants*, London: Circular 7/65, HMSO

DEPARTMENT OF EDUCATION AND SCIENCE (1978-79) (81-82) *School Leavers' Survey*, London: HMSO

DEPARTMENT OF EMPLOYMENT (1990) *Labour Force Survey*, London: Department of Employment

DEPARTMENT OF EMPLOYMENT (1992) *Measure for Measure*, London: Department of Employment

DEPARTMENT OF EMPLOYMENT (1992) *Employment Gazette*, London: Department of Employment, March

DEPARTMENT OF EMPLOYMENT (1994) *Labour Force Survey*, London: Department of Employment

DRIVER, G. (1977) 'Cultural Competence, Social Power and School Achievement, West Indian Secondary School Pupils in the West Midlands', *New Community* 5, (4), pp. 353-359

EGGLESTON, S.J. *et al*, (1981) *In-Service Education in Multicultural Society*, Keele: University of Keele

EQUAL OPPORTUNITIES COMMISSION (1994) *Black Women In The Labour Market: A Research Review*, Manchester: EOC

EYSENCK, H. (1971) *Race, Intelligence and Education*, London: Temple Smith

FOOT, P. (1965) *Immigration and Race in British Politics*, Harmondsworth: Penguin

FRYER, P. (1984) *Staying Power: The History of Black People in Britain*, London: Pluto Press

FULLER, M. (1980) 'Black Girls in a London Comprehensive School' in DEEM, R. (ed) *Schooling For Women's Work*, London: Routledge and Kegan Paul, pp. 47-57

GILLBORN, D. (1990) *Race, Ethnicity and Education*, London: Unwin Hyman

GILROY, P. (1987) *There Ain't No Black in the Union Jack*, London: Hutchinson

GOFFMAN, E. (1976) *Gender Advertisment*, London: Macmillan

GORDON, D. and ROSENBERG, D. (1989) *Daily Racism: The Press and Black People in Britain*, London: The Runnymede Trust

HALL, S., CRITCHER, C., JEFFERSON, T., CLARKE, J. and ROBERTS, B. (1978) *Policing the Crisis: Mugging, the State and Law and Order*, London: Macmillan

HARTMAN, P. and HUSBAND, C. (1974) *Racism and the Media*, London: Davis Poynter

HERRNSTEIN, R. and MURRAY, C. (1994) *The Bell Curve*, New York: Free Press

HOME OFFICE (1968) *Race Relations Act*, London: HMSO

HOME OFFICE (1975) *Racial Discrimination* (Cmnd. 6234) London: HMSO, Para, 57

HOME OFFICE (1975) *Sex Discrimination Act*, London: HMSO

HOME OFFICE (1976) *Race Relations Act*, London: HMSO.

HOUGHTON, V.P. (1966) 'A Report on The Scores of West Indian Immigrants, Children and English Children on an individual Administered test', *Race*, 8, (1)

INSTITUTE OF MANPOWER STUDIES (1989) *Skill Search: Television, Film and Video Industry Employment Patterns and Training Needs, Part One: The Key Facts*, Brighton: University of Sussex, IMS Report No. 171

INSTITUTE OF MANPOWER STUDIES (1990) *Skill Search: Television, Film and Video Industry Employment Patterns and Training Needs, The Final Report*, Brighton: University of Sussex, IMS Report No. 186

JOHNSON, B. (1985) *I Think Of My Mother: Notes On the Life and Times of Claudia Jones*, London: Karia Press

KERNER, O. et al (1968) *Report of the National Advisory Commission on Civil Disorders*, Washington D.C.: US Government Printing Office

KEEBLE, R. (1994) *The Newspaper Handbook*, London: Routledge

LABOUR RESEARCH DEPARTMENT (1985) *Black Workers, Trade Unions and the Law, A Negotiator's Guide*, London: LRD Publication

LITTLE, A., MABEY, C. and WHITAKER, G. (1968) 'The Education of Immigrant Pupils in Primary Schools', *Race*, 9, (4), pp. 439-452

LITTLE, A. (1971) *Performance of Children from Ethnic Minority Backgrounds in Primary School*, London: New Beacon Books

LUSTIG, R. (1990) 'Street-Wise, Cunning, Nothing Short of Hustling by Black and Asian Journalists will force National Papers to Employ more Non-Whites', *Guardian* 12/11/90

MABEY, C. (1986) 'Black Pupils' Achievements in Inner London', *Educational Research*, 28, (3), pp. 163-173

MAC AN GHAILL, M. (1988) *Young, Gifted and Black: Student-Teacher Relations in the Schooling of Black Youth*, Milton Keynes: Open University Press

MACDONALD, I. et al (1989) *Murder in the Playground: the Burnage Report,* London: Longsight Press

MACKINTOSH, N. and MASCIE-TAYLOR, C. (1985) 'The IQ Question' in DES, *Education for All (The Swann Report)*, London: HMSO, Cmnd. 9453, pp. 48-52

METCALF, G. (1970) Introduction to LONG, E. *History of Jamaica, Cass Library of West Indian Studies*, No. 12, London: Frank Cass, p.xi

MIDDLETON, B. (1983) *Factors affecting the Performance of West Indian Boys in a secondary School*, unpublished M.A. thesis, University of York

MILNER, D. (1975) *Children and Race*, Harmondsworth: Penguin

MILNER, D. (1983) *Children and Race: Ten Years On*, London: Ward Lock Educational

MIRZA, H. (1992) *Young, Female and Black*, London: Routledge

NATIONAL ASSOCIATION OF BLACK JOURNALISTS (1988) *Membership Handbook*, Washington: NABJ.

NATIONAL COUNCIL FOR THE TRAINING OF JOURNALISTS (1987) *A History of the National Council for the Training of Journalists*, Epping: NCTJ

NATIONAL FOUNDATION FOR EDUCATIONAL REASEARCH (1966) *Coloured Immigrants' Children: A Survey of Research Studies and Literature on their Educational Problems and Potential in Britain*, Slough: NFER

NATIONAL UNION OF JOURNALISTS (1985) *Conference Report, Broadcasting and Black People*, London: NUJ

NATIONAL UNION OF JOURNALISTS (1986) *Images of Women*, London: NUJ

NATIONAL UNION OF JOURNALISTS (1986) *A Conference Report, Print Journalism And Black People*, London: NUJ

NATIONAL UNION OF JOURNALISTS (1987) *Guidelines on Race Reporting*, London: NUJ

NATIONAL UNION OF JOURNALISTS (1987) *Media Standards*, London: NUJ

NATIONAL UNION OF JOURNALISTS (1987) *Journalists, Gender and Race Equality*, London: NUJ

NATIONAL UNION OF JOURNALISTS (1987) *Journalism Training: Sex and Race Equality*, unpublished paper, London: NUJ

NATIONAL UNION OF JOURNALISTS (1988) *A Conference Report, Black People and the NUJ*, London: NUJ

NATIONAL UNION OF JOURNALISTS (1989) *Careers in Journalism*, London: NUJ

NATIONAL UNION OF JOURNALISTS (1991) *Annual Delegate Meeting Report*, London: NUJ

NATIONAL UNION OF JOURNALISTS (1994) *Membership Survey*, London: NUJ

NATIONAL UNION OF TEACHERS (1989) *Anti-Racism in Education: Guidelines*, London: NUT

NEWSAM, P. (1983) 'Foreword' to ANWAR, M. (Ed.) *Ethnic Minority Broadcasting: A Research Report*, London: Commission for Racial Equality, p.7

NEWSPAPER SOCIETY (1985) *How to Enter Regional Newspapers*, London: The Newspaper Society

NEWSPAPER SOCIETY (1990) *Training for Newspaper Journalism*, London: The Newspaper Society

PAREKH, B. (1978) 'Asians in Britain, Problems or Opportunity' in *Five Views of Multi-Racial Britain: Talks on Race Relations Broadcast by the BBC*, London: Commission for Racial Equality

PAREKH, B. (1986) 'The Politics of Multi-Racial Education in Britain'. Paper presented at the conference, *Education For All: Policies and Practices in Multicultural Education*, Manchester: University of Manchester

PARMAR, P. (1982) 'Gender, Race and Class: Asian Women in Resistance' in CENTRE FOR CONTEMPORARY CULTURAL STUDIES (Eds.) *The Empire Strikes Back*, London: Hutchinson, pp. 236-275

PARMAR, P. (1990) 'Gender, Race and Power: The Challenge to Youth Work Practice' in COHEN, P. *et al* (eds) *Multi-Racist Britain*, London: Macmillan, pp. 190-200

PAYNE, J. (1969) 'A Comparative Study of the Mental Ability of 7 and 8 Year-Old British and West Indian Children in a West Midlands Town', *British Journal of Educational Psychology,* 39, pp. 326-344

PEACH, C. (1968) *West Indian Migration to Britain: A Social Geography,* Oxford: Oxford University Press

PINES, J. (1992) *Black and White in Colour: Black People in British Television Since 1936,* London: BFI Publishing

PLOSKI, H. and WILLIAMS, J. (1989) 'The Black Press and Broadcast Media', in *The Negro Almanack: A Reference Work on the African-American,* Detroit: Gale Research Incorporation, pp. 1252-1296

PREETHI, M. (1987) 'Black Women in British Television Drama – a case of marginal representation', in DAVIES, K. *et al* (eds) *Out of Focus,* London: Women's Press, pp. 42-44

PRYCE, K. (1979) *Endless Pressure: A Study of West Indian Life Styles in Bristol,* Harmondsworth: Penguin

RAINWATER, L. and YANCEY, W. (1967) *The Moynihan Report and the Politics of Controversy,* Cambridge, Mass: The MIT Press

RAMPTON, A. (Chairman) (1981) *West Indian Children in Our Schools: Report of the Committee of Inquiry into the Education of Children from Ethnic Minority Groups,* London: HMSO, Cmnd. 8273

ROSE, E. *et al* (1969) *Colour and Citizenship: A Report on British Race Relations,* Oxford: Oxford University Press

ROWLAND, R. (1982) 'Equal Opportunities at the BBC' in HARTE, J. (ed) *Black People and the Media,* Lewisham: London Borough of Lewisham and the Commission for Racial Equality, pp. 30-37

ROYAL COMMISSION ON THE PRESS (1949) *Report,* London: HMSO, Cmnd. 7700

ROYAL COMMISSION ON THE PRESS (1977) *Final Report,* London: HMSO, Cmnd.6810

SARUP, M. (1986) *The Politics of Multiracial Education,* London: Routledge

SEACOLE, M (1978) *The Wonderful Adventures of Mrs Seacole in Many Lands* edited by Ziggy Alexander and Audrey Dewjee. London: Falling Wall Press

SCHLESINGER, P. (1978) *Putting Reality Together,* London: Constable

SELECT COMMITTEE ON RACE RELATIONS AND IMMIGRATION (1969) *Report,* London: HMSO

SELECT COMMITTEE ON RACE RELATIONS AND IMMIGRATION (1974) *Report, Educational Disadvantage and the Educational Needs of Immigrants,* London: HMSO, Cmnd 5720

SELECT COMMITTEE ON RACE RELATIONS AND IMMIGRATION (1976-77) *Report, The West Indian Community,* HMSO, House of Commons 180, pp. 1-111

SKILLS AND ENTERPRISE NETWORK (1993) *Ethnic Minority Groups Make Good Use of FHE,* Nottingham: Skills and Enterprise Publication (32), pp. 1-4

SMITH, D. (1977) *Racial Disadvantage in Britain,* Harmondsworth: Penguin

STONE, M. (1981) *The Education of the Black Child in Britain,* London: Fontana

STONE, V. (1988) *Pipelines and Dead Ends: Jobs Held by Minorities and Women in Broadcast News,* Columbia, Missouri: University of Missouri

SWANN, M. (Chairman) (1985) *Education for All, Final Report of the Committee of Inquiry into the Education of Children from Ethnic Minority Groups,* London: HMSO, Cmnd. 9453

THOMSON, B. (1988) *Ten Years of ACTT Equality Policies,* London: ACTT

TOMLINSON, S. (1984) 'Black Women in Higher Education – Case Studies of University Women in Britain', in BARTON, L. and WALKER, S. (eds) *Race, Class and Education,* Beckenham: Croom Helm, pp. 66-79

TRADES UNION CONGRESS (1987) *Black Workers: A TUC Charter for Equality of Opportunity*, London: TUC

TRADES UNION CONGRESS (1989) *Equal Opportunities Policies and Procedures: A TUC Guide for Unions as Employers*, London: TUC

TRADES UNION CONGRESS (1991) *Involvement of Ethnic Minority Workers in Trade Unions*, London: TUC

TRADES UNION CONGRESS (1994) *Representation of Black Women in Trade Unions, a checklist for Action*, London: TUC

TRADES UNION CONGRESS (1995) *Black Workers and the Labour Market*, London: TUC

TRADES UNION RESEARCH UNIT (1989) *Survey of New Applicants to the NUJ*, Final Results, London: TURU

TROYNA, B. (1981) *Public Awareness and the Media: A Study of Reporting on Race*, London: Commission for Racial Equality

TUCHMAN, G. (1972) *Making the News: A Study in the Construction of Reality*, New York: The Free Press/Macmillan

TULLOCK, J. (1989) *An Evaluation of PCL's One Year Courses for Black Journalists*, London: Polytechnic of Central London

TULLOCK, J. (1991) *Course Handbook: PCL's Certificate in Periodical Journalism*, London: Polytechnic of Central London

TUMBER, H. (1981) *Television and the Riots*, London: British Film Institute

TUNSTALL, J. (1971) *Journalists at Work. Specialist Correspondents: their news organisations, news sources and competitor-colleagues*, London: Constable

TUNSTALL, J. (1983) *The Media in Britain*, London: Constable

VAN DIJK, T. (1991) *Racism and the Press*, London: Routledge

VAUXHALL COLLEGE (1990) *Access To Journalism*, London: Vauxhall College

WADSWORTH, M. (1985) 'Black Employment in the Broadcasting Industry' in the NATIONAL UNION OF JOURNALISTS (eds) *Broadcasting and Black People, Conference Report*, London: NUJ, pp. 38-50

WADSWORTH, M. (1996) *White Voices, White Faces, White Views*, conference paper

WEAVER, D. and WILHOLT, C. (1986) *The American Journalists*, Indiana: Indiana University Press

WILSON, G. and GUTIERREZ, F. (1985) *Minorities and Media: Diversity and the End of Mass Communications*, Beverly Hills: Sage

WILSON, G. GUTIERREZ, F. (1995) *Race, Multiculturalism and the Media: from Mass to Class Communication*, London: Sage

WRIGHT, C. (1985) 'Who succeeds at school – and who decides?' *Multicultural Teaching*, 4, (1), pp. 17-22

WRIGHT, C. (1987) 'Black Students White Teachers' in TROYNA, B. (ed) *Racial Inequality in Education*, London: Tavistock, pp. 109-126

Newspaper sources

THE BRADFORD TELEGRAPH AND ARGUS 26/11/1985.
CARIBBEAN TIMES 2/4/1991.
CARIBBEAN TIMES 7/5/1991.
THE CORRESPONDENT MAGAZINE 11/11/1990.
COSMOPOLITAN January 1991.
DAILY WORKER 23/6/1948.
DAILY EXPRESS 2/2/1978.
DAILY EXPRESS 13/4/1981.
DAILY EXPRESS 9/3/1995.
DAILY MAIL 8/10/1985.
DAILY MAIL 24/10/1985.
DAILY MAIL 11/4/1981.
DAILY MAIL 13/4/1981.
DAILY MAIL 10/3/1982.
DAILY MAIL 29/10/1986.
DAILY STAR 13/4/1981.
DAILY TELEGRAPH 9/10/1985.
EASTERN EYE 4/6/1991.
EBONY MAGAZINE August 1991.
EMPLOYMENT GAZETTE March 1990.
EVENING STANDARD 21/6/1948.
EVENING STANDARD 29/4/1991.
FINANCIAL TIMES 13/4/1981.
THE GUARDIAN 2/9/1985.
THE GUARDIAN 12/11/1990.
THE INDEPENDENT 3/5/1991.
THE INDEPENDENT 5/12/1995.
THE JOURNAL 29/9/1994.
MANCHESTER GUARDIAN 26/8/1958.
MANCHESTER GUARDIAN 28/8/1958.
MANCHESTER GUARDIAN 5/9/1958.
NEW YORK TIMES 24/12/1978.
OBSERVER COLOUR MAGAZINE 21/2/1988.
THE SUN 13/4/1981.
THE SUN 11/4/1981.
THE SUN 24/10/1981.
THE SUN 11/3/1982.
THE SUN 29/4/1991.
THE SUNDAY TELEGRAPH 10/3/1996.
THE SUNDAY TIMES 13/7/1983.
THE SUNDAY TIMES 21/4/1968.
THE SUNDAY EXPRESS 21/4/1968.
THE TIMES EDUCATIONAL SUPPLEMENT 26/4/1968.
THE TIMES EDUCATIONAL SUPPLEMENT 31/1/1992.
THE VOICE 23/4/1991.
THE VOICE 4/6/1991.
THE VOICE 7/5/1991.

Index